THE
TERRACOTTA
GARDENER

To Dominique

THE TERRACOTTA GARDENER

JIM KEELING

*Photographs of terracotta displays
by Andrew Lawson*

Trafalgar Square Publishing
NORTH POMFRET, VERMONT

First published in the United States of America in 1990
by Trafalgar Square Publishing, North Pomfret, Vermont 05053

ISBN 0 943955 22 X

LOC 89–51251

AN EDDISON · SADD EDITION
Edited, designed and produced by
Eddison Sadd Editions Limited
St Chad's Court, 146B King's Cross Road
London WC1X 9DH

Phototypeset by Bookworm Typesetting, Manchester, England
Origination by Columbia Offset, Singapore
Printed in Hong Kong

CONTENTS

*"Throwing" is an ancient craft. The techniques used at Whichford Pottery
to make these giant flowerpots are those that have been used for centuries.*

CHAPTER ONE

THE MAKING OF TERRACOTTA

A whole tome on flowerpots? Surely the man is . . .". But wait! Fifteen years ago, an ardent young potter fresh from Cambridge University, I would have been rattled and hastily agreed. The subject was no subject at all.

At first, if I admitted as a potter to making flowerpots, I could always feel the half-formed retort "But what do you really make?" The truth is that I did not set out to make terracotta; we found each other by happy accident. I wanted to make highly decorated earthenware, inspired by the early Islamic pottery I had dug up in Persia as an archaeologist. But first I wanted to learn to "throw" on the wheel, and the only pottery near my parents' house with a job to offer was A. Harris & Sons at Wrecclesham, near Farnham in Surrey, founded in 1874. I worked there with two old potters and one other apprentice while the ramshackle buildings leaked and crumbled all around us. The old brick floors undulated down a gentle slope in the gloom of the drying sheds, and carefully placed pots caught the drips upstairs. Nothing had changed for generations, and all that was made were flowerpots.

Once begun, I found the task of mastering the deceptively simple techniques used in making terracotta ever more fascinating. Being an archaeology and history graduate, I was intrigued to find the bones of a tradition stretching back to the dawn of recorded time, yet surfacing quite recognizable and remarkably unchanged in the present.

...*"Do not grudge
To pick out treasures from an earthen pot.
The worst speak something good"*.

George Herbert (from *The Church Porch* published 1633)

The first potters

Potters, together with weavers, were the first manufacturers; men who took a raw material and by processing it produced something quite different, man-made. There are antecedents – the late Stone Age flint knappers and axe polishers were specialist craftsmen exporting all over Europe from various centres, and agriculture itself reorders nature – but pottery involves many skills and many processes, and some quite sophisticated machinery.

The great revolution in pottery-making was the invention of the wheel. If you can keep a lump of clay spinning round long enough, by squeezing and pinching it you can transform the circular energy into vertical movement of the clay itself – a sort of magic that never fails to mesmerize anyone watching from the first day to this. The original wheel would have been very simple, probably just a heavy flywheel which itself was also the wheelhead on which the pot was made, a type still

This sixteenth-century woodcut shows the different processes of pottery-making. In the background a man digs the clay, and others chop firewood and stoke the kilns. Plaster moulds and finished pots sit under the cracked windows.

commonly used in India. Later potters' wheels had elongated the central shaft and added a separate wheelhead, allowing the potter to "kick" on the flywheel while sitting down alongside the head. This type is still used all over Europe and the Middle East.

In England a further refinement was developed in the eighteenth century whereby a crank or double bend was put in the shaft between the flywheel and wheelhead, allowing a foot-operated kick-bar to be added. This is much less tiring and more consistent than kicking the flywheel direct. Nowadays, the motive power usually comes from electric motors; but the technique of actually forming the clay on a rotating wheelhead always remains the same.

The potter's wheel is a very efficient machine. Before its invention, potters could hand coil perhaps a couple of dozen pots a day. Now in the same time and with a little extra skill, they can produce hundreds.

Who invented the first potter's wheel? We know that he lived just over five thousand years ago somewhere in the Fertile Crescent, the cradle of civilization centred on the Tigris-Euphrates basin and roughly speaking within the area of modern Iraq.

Today, the same area is an endless tedium of flat aridity, puckered only by the mounds or "tells" of vanished settlements. The irrigation systems, so skilfully laid out thousands of years ago, were destroyed by Hulagu the Mongul in AD 1258 and the Arabs were too far past their creative zenith ever to restore them.

Writing was first thought of here at about the same time as the wheel and for thousands of years the two crafts were closely linked. The cuneiform script was "written" by pressing a wedge-shaped stylus into wet clay tablets, later baked in the sun.

I feel sure that it was the same development in human consciousness that brought forth both writing and the potter's wheel. Writing allows the logical ordering of sound into shapes, apparent chaos made coherent, just as the repetitive nature of the wheel encourages the logical development of both shapes and processes. The industrial revolution has made us wary of the production line, but as a thrower myself I can easily imagine the wonderful sense of mastery that those early potters felt, as they looked down the gleaming rows of fresh pots standing on the earth.

The terracotta tradition can trace its lineage

Affectionately known as a "slave" wheel, this type was an English invention using the latest technology from the early Industrial Revolution. The wheel had become a sophisticated tool, and a spare wheelhead lies to the left.

straight back to these first beginnings. Later developments in pottery techniques have often been to do with glazing, firing temperature and refinements of the clay body, but unglazed earthenware owes nothing to these. A Bronze Age potter from four thousand years ago would recognize almost all the ways of "making" that I use at Whichford today.

Modern man finds it hard to keep in touch with his past. New technology and machinery have been applied to pottery manufacture as much as to other industry. Automated production processes now dominate the spirit and design of most pottery.

Michael Cardew, a leader in the English Crafts Pottery revival this century, used to point out that the simpler the processes the easier it would be for a craftsman to stay true both to himself and his tradition. More complicated technology has such a strong internal logic that it is hard for an individual to do anything other than serve that logic. It is easy to illustrate this with contemporary examples from Stoke-on-Trent, where the last forty years have seen the demise of a fine tradition by blind obeisance to the twin gods of modernization and "economic" rationalization.

Crete ancient and modern

Modern Iraq has little left to remind you of its early civilizations, but by the end of the third millennium BC the area's cultural influence had spread via the Mediterranean all over Europe. Two rival empires had developed, one centred in Egypt, the other in Crete. It is in Crete, under the vastness of Mount Ida, that my story really begins.

Among the grey crags of Mount Ida, Zeus was born; on its slopes King Minos hunted wild boar while Ariadne fell in love with Theseus and helped him to outwit the fearsome Minotaur. On Crete you are never far from myth and the Ancient World seems very near.

At the Minoan museum in Iraklion most of the exhibits are pottery. They have a strange, fresh quality. The men who made these pots were breaking new, unknown ground. Never before had such sophistication been seen either in complexity and variety of form, use of colour, or

The labyrinth at Knossos was full of vast jars, used to store olive oil and wine. The stone cists in the floor held precious things, alabaster vases, gold, tools, and weapons, safe in the dark maze of passages.

In pre-industrial societies pottery was close to agriculture. Even today these kilns at Thrapsano in Crete are fired with dried cake from the local olive press, and pottery is only made during the summer months when the potters' farms need little attention.

decorative subtlety. Going round the showcases, you suddenly come across a familiar shape or pattern, and gradually you realize that much of what is now taken for granted in pottery design was first established by these potters from Kamares four thousand years ago.

Visiting the Minoan palace at Knossos it is impossible to miss the vast storage jars. There are enough to store the tribute of an empire, and they line the cellars, room after room, a labyrinthine maze of passages. On some jars you can still see cracking and smoke marks, reminders of the vast fire, fuelled by the olive oil they contained, which destroyed the palace one spring day about 1450 BC.

Crete is a strange place. It has vast, harsh mountains, and also rich foothills and plains. The empires of the eastern Mediterranean have all ruled it in turn, but never easily. They built a coastal fortress maybe, a harbour or a garrison post, but the old Crete continued all around.

When I visited the potteries at Marguerites in Crete recently in June, I felt this continuity with the past more strongly than ever. It is one of the two villages in Crete where large pots are still made, and I had visited the other, Thrapsano, two years before, one wet October. If you buy a Cretan pot in England it will probably be from the Thrapsano cooperative, where they still make large pots in the traditional way, using some modern machinery and new buildings. This is sensible but not particularly exciting.

Marguerites is quite different. It is a beautiful village, with two squares and little alleys winding up a steep hill. They obviously had a prosperous time last century which has left many beautiful dressed-stone doorways, their arches Greek blue with heavy doors, giving glimpses of hidden gardens or cool, dark hallways.

A wander round the old potting district above the village is like a visit to the Bronze Age. Nothing has changed since the time of Daedalus, as far as I could judge, either in technique, form or organization.

The potteries, I was told, were up the hill, towards the mountain. So off I trudged, keeping the wide gorge with its orange-grove floor and cypress sides to my right. It is a pleasant road, with

olive trees all around, a few small wheatfields, and Mount Ida always behind them. First I saw a kiln. They are known as "Roman" kilns, but really they should be called "Minoan" as the Romans just used what was there already. They are built with heavy stone walls, lined smooth inside with a "clam" of clay and sand. Internally they are round with vertical sides. A third of the way up a floor raises the pots above the fire. The top is open to the sky, so the loaded pots are covered with broken potsherds during a firing to hold back the heat inside the kiln. The biggest kilns are 10 feet across the inside, the smallest 3 foot.

The whole way up the road are dilapidated kilns and beside each one a ruined hut, all set in small compounds bounded by stone walls. At last I arrived at a hut which was not a ruin, or falling in, beside a kiln that was half filled with new pots. I ducked into the shadow of the hut and stood before an old man, quietly kicking round an ancient wheel. He was making the spout for an olive-oil lamp.

If you turned off the radio (which thankfully Costas did) and removed his baseball hat, I could not have guessed the century. In one corner stood the wheel and the clay, primitive shelves covered

At Marguerites in Crete, there are craftsmen who work in ways unchanged for thousands of years. This flat-roofed hut stands in a compound beside two simple kilns.

the walls, and smaller pots, water jars, saucers and cups were stacked under the far window. No electricity, no concrete; only a wooden table and a chair. Outside, everything was equally simple. Two kilns, one for small ware, one for larger pots, backed on the hut. A couple of trees sheltered an old bed to take care of the hot afternoons, and behind these lay the clay preparation area.

Old potteries are always near their clay sources. At Marguerites the pits are a couple of miles away up in the hills, and the potteries owe their exact siting to a rather unusual feature – a great limestone slab. It formed the slope I had walked up from the village, and lies just under the surface like an unbroken layer of ancient concrete. The ingenious potters used it to help prepare their clay.

Two different local clays are used, mixed in different proportions depending on the size of pot to be made. It is not difficult to get the clays bone dry, when they are spread out on to the hard flat limestone and broken up by beating with an olive-wood hammer. The powder thus gained is

Large pots have to be built up in stages. The lower parts are allowed to stiffen slightly, before a new section is added, so that they become strong enough to hold the weight above.

put into old pots, or into tanks hewn out of the stone slab, and there mixed with water into a "slip" or slurry. To get the worst impurities out, it is then ladled through a sieve (in the old days made of basketwork) and allowed to run down the gently sloping limestone slab, forming a thick layer of mud. Next day this mud will be dry enough to roll up into a heap, where it is trodden or punched to mix the hard and the soft, before being stored in the hut. There are variations, but all potters use the same stages to refine and mix their clay.

In primitive societies, craft skills are often shared more communally than is usual nowadays, when being a craftsman is a full-time specialist job. At Marguerites, every family used to have its own compound. Until the war in 1940 everyone was a potter, and the family worked as a group just as Costa's wife now slip decorates his pots and helps him load the kilns.

But, as in many primitive societies, being a craftsman was not their only job. I remember once walking for half a day near the Atlantic coast of Morocco looking for a potter, and when I finally found his village they thought I was mad – did I not know that he always went fishing at this time of year? It is just the same at Marguerites. The potting is seasonal, backing up agriculture.

This ties in well with the weather. Pots are only made in the hotter months when agriculture is slack, not in the wet winter when they would never dry out and the olives and pistachios need tending, and the other crops have to be planted.

There is one last remarkable element in the Marguerites compounds and it is now unique to Crete, though formerly other islands used it too. Outside each hut is a line of wheels and on these are made the vast storage jars like those in the Palace at Knossos. There are many technical problems making very large pots. When throwing a single lump of clay, the height of the pot formed will be limited in height to the length of your arm, and more than about half a hundredweight of clay is very unwieldy, especially on a kickwheel. So how are these jars, sometimes 6 feet high and weighing several hundredweight, made? They are built up in sections.

The Cretan way is this, and it uses the harsh climate as an aid: first, you make a 30-foot-long

*Thrapsano lies in the centre of Crete, surrounded by olive groves and pistachio farms. In the background rises Mount Dicte,
where Rhea gave birth to Zeus in a deep cave hidden from the savagery of his father Cronos.*

Siragopoulis Manolis from Marguerites in Crete rolls out a coil of clay to form another section of a pot (left). He pinches it onto the slowly turning pot, then he wets the new coil and throws it up to form the wall or rim of the pot (right).

step, 18 inches high with ten niches in it. Into each of these niches you set a simple turned wooden wheelhead. You then need two men to make these pots, the potter who stands on the step with the wheelhead at his feet and a "slave" who squats below him, turning one wheelhead after another as each is used in turn.

A base section is thrown on each wheel. Because of the great heat, by the time the tenth base is thrown, the first will be getting quite stiff, dry enough to add a sausage of clay around the rim in a "coil". Unlike a true coil pot, this coil is put on much thicker than the wall of the pot – it is about 3 inches in diameter – and is then itself "thrown", forming another 6 or 8 inches of pot. As the pot grows, the "slave's" job becomes, surprisingly, easier, as the increased weight of clay gives added momentum to the spinning wheel. Once the second section is finished on all ten pots, the process begins again with the first pot, another coil is added and so on. Up to six sections may be used, the last always being left thick to form the rim.

There are various tricks involved. First the clay must be just right – quite wet and sticky, and of a type well able to stand rapid drying without cracking. The rim of the previous section must be scratched and wettened before adding the new piece. A length of string is also wound twice round the old section, just below the rim, to prevent splitting as the new coil is added. This is removed once the coil has been thrown.

Decoration is added section by section as the pots grow in height. Very wet clay – we call it "squibber" at Whichford – is dabbed on the pot, then thrown into shape with a wet sponge for horizontal rings or shaped freehand for more elaborate decoration. All the designs I saw in Crete would have been recognized by their Minoan inventors, although the repertoire is now much more limited.

But changing times have almost destroyed the old tradition. Oil and wine are now stored in steel or concrete bins and the many other specialist uses for large pots, like vats for tanning or laundry, have gone. Only a tiny handful of potters still carry on making the large pots, and their purpose is quite new – flowerpots. The old shapes have been adapted and northern Europeans, Japanese and Americans now buy the pots the Cretans themselves no longer want.

There is nothing new in using pots made for other purposes as flowerpots. In fact for thousands of years that is what flowerpots usually were – old, broken or spare cooking pots and storage vessels. It is only comparatively recently that gardeners started commissioning special pots for their own needs.

This makes the early history of flowerpots very puzzling. The Minoans often painted flowers on pots, but there are no Minoan pots which we can definitely say were made for flowers.

Egypt and the first pleasure gardens

Across the sea in Egypt we have a much fuller picture of daily life than in Crete, where earthquakes and damp winters have destroyed so much. It was the Egyptians who began pleasure gardening, and pot plants have always been a decoration rather than an agricultural necessity. There are many wall paintings in Egyptian tombs depicting garden scenes, including plants in pots. One from El-Bersheh (Fourth/Fifth Dynasty) shows a vine arbour and vegetable garden, with flowerpots lining a wall. They are planted with single conical shrubs and perhaps corms like young gladioli. Later we know that Rameses III (1198–1166 BC) was a great gardener and introduced many new plants. In his reign trees and shrubs were often grown in decorated earthenware vases.

Egyptian gardens were formal, and established the tradition of separate compartments divided by trees, arbours or walls.

They used their flowerpots to point up the symmetry of the design, on corners of central ponds or in straight lines along a path or wall. This way of gardening spread all over the Near East, especially to Greece, and from there to Rome and thus to our own culture.

In ancient Greece, Aphrodite, the Goddess of Love, was the patroness of flowers and gardens. Flowery groves were kept as sacred homes for female divinities and their sprites, and the goddess was often "violet-crowned". It was within the cult of Aphrodite that a strange ceremony developed – the Adonis gardens.

The Adonis gardens of classical antiquity

Adonis was a Cypriot prince, and he was so handsome that Aphrodite fell madly in love with him. Unfortunately, so did Persephone, Queen of the Underworld, and in her jealousy she told Aphrodite's favourite paramour, the warlike Ares, of his lover's infidelity. Enraged, Ares turned

Vine arbour and plants in pots, based on a wall painting at El-Bersheh.

A painting on a Greek vase shows the two broken halves of an amphora turned into ritual flowerpots. Eros hands Aphrodite, naked to symbolize her deity, a freshly planted pot which she carries up a ladder to the roof.

himself into a huge wild boar and fell upon Adonis while he was out hunting, mortally wounding him. Where his fine blood fell, wild anemonies sprang up. He soon died, and descended into Hades and the arms of Persephone. Aphrodite was distraught, and pestered Zeus for justice. Finally, he ruled that Adonis should divide his time equally between the Upper and Lower Worlds. Six months a year he should spend with Aphrodite, and the other six months with Persephone. Thus he came to symbolize the changing seasons of summer and winter.

By the sixth century BC the death and revival of Adonis, or Thamuz as he was called further east, were widely celebrated all over the eastern Mediterranean. At Midsummer, for instance, the women of Athens would set up an image of Adonis on their flat rooftops, the while singing dirges over the death of Aphrodite's lover. All around the statue they placed flowerpots filled with soil, and these were then ceremonially sown with the seeds of fennel and lettuce and ears of barley and wheat. The plantings soon sprang up but were never watered, and so died quickly. The early and inevitable death of the vegetation echoed the fate of the beautiful youth Adonis.

At first, this was an unofficial cult like May Day, but by the time of Christ it had become so popular that it was a great public festival, celebrated with much pomp. Shakespeare mentions Adonis gardens in *Henry IV Part 1*, and so does Milton in *Paradise Lost* and Spenser in *The Faerie Queen*. Adonis gardens are so often mentioned in literature because they came to stand for things of small importance and short-lived pleasures.

But in this cult can be seen the beginnings of a gardening in pots that grew in popularity over many centuries. Soon the adornment provided by planted pots was being adopted for its own sake, not just for the Adonis cult, and the pots began to remain in situ and planted throughout the year. Theophrastus is quite definite about this in his botanical works written about 300 BC. Soon afterwards Hiero, King of Syracuse, had an enormous ship built for him, designed by a certain engineer called Archimedes. His theories about the displacement of water were certainly put to the test – the ship had a garden on its huge deck with lead-lined flowerbeds and rows of large flowerpots holding ivies and grape vines trained over pergolas to shade the decks and gangways.

Three centuries later in Imperial Rome, the Adonis garden had become a thing of wonder. When Apollonius of Tyrenia, the worker of miracles, had an audience with Domitian in the Palatine Palace, the Emperor awaited him in the court of Adonis. As Apollonius described it, "This court was adorned with flowers just as the Assyrians plant them on the roofs in honour of Adonis." Apollonius had travelled all over the Near East, including Syria where the cult of Thamuz originated. His comments show that flowerpots were then in common use throughout the eastern Mediterranean. At the palace of Domitian, the urns were set as a decoration round the roof of a pillared court, and excavations at Pompeii, destroyed a decade earlier in AD 79, show similar layouts.

Pliny the Younger, like his uncle killed during the eruption of Vesuvius, was a great writer on gardening and had fine Tuscan estates himself. He loved the effect of the flowerpots which decorated the roofs and balconies in Rome, and likened them to the gardens of the Hesperides, the garden of Alcinous, and the hanging gardens of Semiramis, "all of them exceedingly wonderful".

Two hundred years later, the temples of Venus

Artists often depict potters, but not always accurately. In this Roman wall painting the heavy flywheel is correct, but the painter is not quite sure what a potter does with his hands.

(the Roman equivalent of Aphrodite) still needed flowerpots, as we know from this story. Seville, in Spain, had a particularly beautiful shrine to Venus, and one day its priestess went to buy some flowerpots from the local potter. He was a poor man, and the retail sales were looked after by his daughters, Justa and Rufina. The priestess tried to drive a hard bargain and an argument followed. Insults were exchanged and the recent conversion of the girls to Christianity no doubt made matters worse. Anyway, that night the sisters were caught in the act of defiling the temple by destroying the sacred statues and were duly sentenced to death by the Roman Governor. They are now the patron saints of Seville and their attributes are an array of earthenware pots.

Roman gardens and terracotta

Pliny's account of his estate at Tusci could easily be a description of an early Renaissance villa in the same place. The Roman aesthetic is a synthesis of the influences from Egypt, Persia and especially the Hellenistic World. Because this is part of the heritage of the Western world, we can easily recognize the lay-out of Pliny's villa. You walk from its inside courtyards, through upper terraces enclosing lawns edged by clipped box hedges, down steps into the lower garden with its walls and vistas, and rest on its shady benches beside the marble fountains.

Roman gardeners were innovators as well as borrowers. They invented topiary, derived from the *Ars Topiaria* whose aim was to illustrate a theme using natural elements. Originally the theme would have been sacred – perhaps a boundary stone surmounted by a Hermes would have ivy and myrtle trained around it representing Bacchus and Venus. The art became so developed that Pliny records whole scenes cut out from box and cypress showing huntsmen and their quarry, or even fleets of ships.

Together with topiary, the Romans knew much about the subtle arts of pruning and grafting. They also knew of the benefits of applied heat, and invented the precursors to the greenhouse, using steam to heat hothouses with mica windows to produce flowers throughout the year.

In pottery, too, the Romans developed many new techniques. They had huge terracotta work-shops using slave labour which produced millions of bricks, tiles, pipes and pots every year for several centuries. The great brick dome of the Pantheon finished in AD 123, is one of the wonders of the world. Few buildings have ever used more bricks, unless you count the Great Wall of China built two hundred years before or the massive Ziggurat at Ur of the Chaldees; but both of these are largely composed of unbaked brick whereas the Pantheon uses only burned brick.

The word "terracotta" is derived from the Latin *terra cocta* meaning "baked earth". The Romans used it to describe all the heavy earthenware produced in those brick factories. Significantly, the word also covers Etruscan sarcophagi, the relief work on which is widely copied. There were often scenes depicting figures or swags of fruit and flowers in bas-relief all round the coffins. The Greek influence is strong; and some of the designs have a richness which points further East, along the desert trade routes through the Parthian Empire to India itself.

Decoration on terracotta was often modelled laboriously by hand. The Romans also developed the use of moulds, again using Greek and Egyptian ideas. Smearing clay onto an outside "former" is an easy way of making a pot, and examples of vessels

made in this way using a basket are found from the earliest times. In the seventh century BC the Greeks had begun to use moulds to reproduce sophisticated terracotta figurines, and by Roman times life-size sculptures were being made using complicated moulds in many sections. These moulds were usually constructed from fired clay, and relief decoration was incorporated in them, the motifs being cut into the mould and so raised proud on the finished article. Plaster, although rough and short lived, was also occasionally used. The main centres of production were in the Rhone valley and this Gaulish pottery can be found all over the Empire. Called *terra sigillata*, or "Arrentine ware" after the town of Arrezzo which was the earliest production centre, it is usually burnished red and was made on the wheel by "throwing" a lump of clay up the inside of a centred mould.

In my opinion this is the first example of really boring pottery. I find that much Roman art suffers from the same dullness, perhaps because it was made by slaves ordered to copy and produce on demand. There is a feeling of hollowness which reflects the growing spiritual and moral vacuum of the times, when emperors were worshipped along-side the old gods. Later Eastern Empire and Byzantine work is suddenly full of vigour as

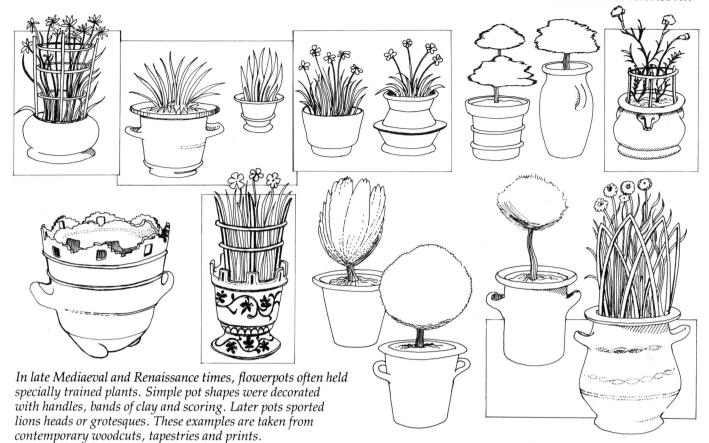

In late Mediaeval and Renaissance times, flowerpots often held specially trained plants. Simple pot shapes were decorated with handles, bands of clay and scoring. Later pots sported lions heads or grotesques. These examples are taken from contemporary woodcuts, tapestries and prints.

craftsmen once more glorify God and breathe fresh life into the old motifs, drawing renewed inspiration from the insights of Christianity. It is tempting to draw parallels in our own century with mass production design using "wage-slaves", where the motive forces are the purely secular demands of a profit-orientated materialism which will not acknowledge the spiritual dimension in creation.

We are so used to Roman design and ideas resuscitated by the early Renaissance that it is easy to forget their stormy passage through a thousand years. The Dark Ages loom after Rome's collapse, and, despite their great desire to be Romanized, successive waves of Gothic invaders destroyed much. Early casualties were the great extended gardens of the Senatorial villas, in times when such public displays of opulence became unwise. Society became more insular and inward-looking and the towns decayed. With them declined the great terracotta works, until by the sixth century AD little of the tradition was left. It was not to be revived in Italy until the fifteenth century.

The Middle Ages
Throughout the many changes in the Middle Ages, flowerpots always remained in use. The new force of Islam took over Roman garden design and added fresh ideas from the Middle East, especially Persia. Persian *Pairidaeza* parks reflected the ideal communion between the four sacred elements of earth, air, fire and water (hence the meaning of the Greek *paradeisos* – a state of blessedness, like an ideal garden), and were always enclosed and symmetrical.

Their formal simplicity gave great prominence to accessories, including flowerpots. These would stand at the intersection of paths or line the edge of a canal, and if flowers were used at all in the Islamic garden, they would be in these pots. The flowers used were often chosen for their scent and included aromatic shrubs and herbs. The pots were usually simple, and large enough for only one plant, and often made up in quantity what they lacked in subtlety.

The fine Arab gardens of Sicily greatly impressed the Normans when they conquered the island in AD 1091, and inspired a new interest in gardening. In Western Europe the next three hundred years saw a gradual increase in gardening knowledge beyond the confines of the monastic orders. Many new species were introduced. With the Italian Renaissance in the fifteenth century this gradual change culminated in the birth of modern gardening.

The Italian Renaissance

Leon Battista Alberti was a true Renaissance man – architect, artist, author, musician and gardener. He laid down principles for the "Italian" style of garden design which can still be recognized today. He tried to copy the style of classical antiquity, and drew heavily on Pliny and other authors (incidentally often preserved by the Arabs in translation). But when he banishes coloured flowers to terracotta pots, he is perhaps more Arab than Roman. A description of the garden designed by him for Giovanni Rucellai at Villa Quarachi, near Florence, includes a walled-in garden with paths and a small meadow full of flowerpots containing Damascus violets, marjoram, basil and other sweet-smelling herbs. In other gardens he recommends fountains surrounded by pots and amphorae full of flowers. The villa of Cosimo di Medici at Careggi had just such a fountain, and also walks lined with terra-

In gardens of the Italian Renaissance citrus trees in huge terracotta pots often lined the edges of walks or ponds. In this representation of the Villa d'Este, Tivoli, there are three ponds, each one surrounded by two dozen pots.

Revelling in the newly-found laws of perspective, Carlo Crivelli (c. 1435–93) depicts the Annunciation in a Florentine palace. Flowerpots abound and behind the peacock are terracotta panels, modelled in the style of the della Robbia workshop.

cotta urns, though here they were filled with orange and lemon trees.

No other potted plant has been treated with more reverence than the citrus tree. It even had a type of building especially designed for it – the orangery. Small wonder it is so, for there are few pleasanter sights than orange and lemon trees festooned with fruit, some ripe and some green. Citrus trees are easily killed by frost. When the northern Italians took up their culture from the Arabs, they were forced to plant them in movable containers so that they could take them into orangeries during the winter. In fact, they thrive in pots, growing into magnificent specimens which can live for over a hundred years.

Orangeries are not always as splendid as the glass-fronted edifices of the eighteenth and nineteenth centuries. I have seen a much simpler one near Siena, just a lean-to building backed on to a high wall. A pantile roof slopes down to an arched outside wall – the openings are quite small and the whole building relatively dark. Every few feet of its great length is a small brick plinth, one for each treasured pot, some of them more than two hundred years old. In the corner is a strange two-wheeled cart, its solid floor ending wedge-shaped, so that when the whole contraption is tilted it can be slipped under the edge of a pot. Four men and various ropes are needed to bring the pots in or out.

The potteries in Impruneta, near Florence, make a wide range of garden ornaments as well as flowerpots (above). Before it is fired, terracotta may vary in colour from grey through yellow to dark red depending on its source. It turns orange in the firing. In an old workshop, like this one in Impruneta, everything takes on the colour of the clay.

Orange trees in pots can survive frost, for indeed these old orangeries only keep out the worst of the weather. The secret is to keep the root ball barely moist when there is a risk of freezing, for if the roots are wet the effect of the cold will be fatal.

No one can be certain what the orange pots in Cosimo di Medici's gardens looked like, but it is known that following Alberti's ideas they were very numerous, and were probably very large. I often wonder what would have happened to the flowerpot tradition without the orange tree and its need for plenty of root space. I suspect the pots would have remained smaller and more homely like those in Roman, Islamic or Gothic gardens.

The Florentine terracotta Renaissance

The mid-fifteenth century marked the beginning of a great resurgence of terracotta making in Tuscany, and many of the modern kiln sites around Florence and Siena date from then. Alberti published *De Architectura* in 1445, and Cosimo di Medici's gardens were begun in 1457. In 1443 a certain Luca della Robbia caused a sensation in Florence when he unveiled a tympanum of the Resurrection in the sacristy of Santa Maria del Fiere. It was made of tin-glazed terracotta.

Luca della Robbia had originally been apprenticed a goldsmith, moving as a teenager into marble carving. But by his early thirties he realized that there was no money to be had in stone carving as it took too long. So he experimented with clay and with glazes using "tin, lithange, antimony and other materials" to "render his works practically imperishable". Giorgio Vasari, in his *Lives*, written a century later, credits him with inventing his own glazes, but for the construction and firing of his complicated works he would certainly have drawn heavily on existing traditions in the making of bricks, oil jars, washing tubs and other large terracotta pieces.

Soon he was running a large family business which exported all over Europe mainly bas-relief panels, but also the first free-standing terracotta figures since classical times. This highly productive workshop made fancy terracotta pots for the new gardens of the rich. These are the originals for many of the designs still used today. They also made *pavimenti* flooring bricks; when Raphael designed an ornate floor using white and red brick patterns for the Appartamento Borgia in the Vatican, they were supplied by the della Robbia workshop in Florence.

Today, in the hills just south of Florence, at Impruneta, workshops can be found still using kilns and buildings founded in this Golden Age. Unlike in Crete, the work is all done inside, under high arches which create cool, dark space. The clay is refined by beating it into a fine powder and then mixing it with just enough water. Its grey colour has long since smothered everything, and in the older workshops the dust piles softly up on dim heaps of forgotten machinery parts, or moulds, or heaven-knows-what half-broken relics.

But the tradition is very much alive. While machinery has taken over the mass production of a few plainer pots, there are still a good number of small family firms making them by hand.

The oldest method used is a variation of hand coiling. A clay base is flattened out onto a wooden or pottery "bat" which stays like a round tray under the pot enabling it to be moved around while still wet. The potter then twists and thumbs a coil of clay onto the base as he walks backwards round it. This coil is then smoothed up and another coil added. As in Crete the potter may need to work on several pots at once to allow them to dry slightly before adding the upper coils. But here there is no circular motion from a wheel to help the potter, so, in order to achieve a relatively smooth rim, or to put on a band of decoration, he has to shuffle backwards around the pot at a most alarming and dizzying rate.

This simple technique, which requires only a sponge of water and a wooden scraper to execute, produces beautiful pots. But once a coil is in place you cannot alter or correct its outside shape, so there is great skill involved in creating and following the correct outline as the pot is gradually built up. The nature of the process leaves the pot with a pleasant waywardness, a definite proportion which is yet imprecisely and swiftly finished. I am reminded of Vasari's astute comments on Luca della Robbia, that things "born in an instant in the heat of inspiration express the idea of their author in a few strokes, while on the other hand too much effort and diligence sometimes sap the vitality and powers of those who never know when to leave off."

Decoration on these pots is nowadays simple. Above or between the applied bands of decoration swags or rosettes are sometimes added from small "sprig" moulds, which are first filled with clay and then offered up to the dampened pot. In former times more complex modelling was often added. Swags composed of individual leaves and fruit, each rolled out quickly in the hand and pushed together to build up the desired shape, would hang between highly ornate satyrs' heads or grotesque handles. These days this work is not much done: it is considered too time-consuming and costly.

Moulding has always played an important part in these Florentine workshops. The della Robbias soon resorted to making moulds of their more popular lines, adding by hand only the finishing details. I was told that many of the most ornate designs now available in Impruneta were developed in moulds during the eighteenth and nineteenth centuries, using plaster of Paris rather than the terracotta of earlier times. This new plaster was first refined from the gypsums of Montmartre in the 1740s, and gave more detailed casts than any previous material.

Hand filling these large ornate moulds is a skilled job and takes much time and effort. The mould is first dusted with fired clay powder, this parting the finished pot from the mould better than raw dust. The clay is then coiled into place inside the mould. To fill the lower portion of the mould, the potter has to lean right inside it, and, as each new coil is added, it is beaten up the side of the mould, pressing it firmly onto the last coil and thinning the wall of the pot to the desired thickness. After a few hours the plaster mould is taken off in its various pieces, leaving only the work of removing blemishes, or "fettling". The advantages of this hand pressing technique are that any shape can be made, in particular squares, rectangles and oblongs, and any amount of decoration can be applied. The effect of this richness is sometimes overwhelming, but handled with care it can also be very pleasing.

The kilns used in Impruneta are square, and up to 15 feet across. They are a kind of "cross draught" kiln, and trap hot air inside them much more efficiently than the old Roman or later updraught kilns, using technology that reached Europe from China through Persia. Traditionally the kilns would have been fired with wood from the outer Tuscan hills. Now faggots are used only to raise the final temperature and oil does the main work. Some large works have converted to propane, which is a pity as the cleaner flame fails to bring out the subtle colour variations which make Impruneta pots so particularly beautiful.

The variety in the output of these Tuscan workshops is astounding. At one end, they still turn out *pavimenti*, and the Roman pantile system, with its wide flat under-tile and curved over-tile. At the other extreme, the largest workshops have resident sculptors, usually striving in vain to recall the skills of the della Robbias, making one-off sculptures to commission. In between is the main body of production which, since oil jars are no longer in demand, is now flowerpots. One man makes them several yards high, with full complements of gigantic swags and life-size acanthus leaves, building them up over several weeks and eventually working off scaffolding. More usually, a yard across is considered big and most of the production is between 12 and 24 inches in diameter. Most of the workshops both build by hand and hand press in moulds, and include various statues and plaques in their repertoire.

Unlike most traditional potters, the men and women at Impruneta have no doubts as to the worth of their work. I am reminded of Renaissance craftsmen by their quiet assurance, derived, surely, from the knowledge that they make an excellent product which is still much in demand. These are not the landless peasant potters of Andalusia, or the farmer potters of Crete, but master artisans whom a prince might easily consult while planning his garden or designing his tomb.

England in the seventeenth century

With the flowerpot comfortably ensconced at the beginnings of our modern gardening tradition, all around pools and paths, emblazoned with the arms of dukes and ever more fanciful in shape and decoration, I want finally to look at England, and trace the growth of the "Country Pottery" tradition in which I work.

The story continues from Italy, because although it took two hundred years for the insular English to hear of, digest and adopt the new ideas of the Renaissance, they came to dominate England too.

Some years ago I was commissioned by the National Trust to make a series of urns for Ham House, near Richmond, to add the finishing touches to the restoration of Sir Thomas Browne's garden design for the house of the 1680s. We could not be certain what the original line of pots, prominently placed along a vast terrace in front of the house, would have looked like. This started me thinking along two lines – where did the influences on pot design come from at that time; and who in England was making the elaborate pieces which contemporary records tell us would have been used to adorn such gardens.

At first I looked for influences in earlier pieces of pottery, signs of a tradition, pots to copy or adapt. But I had forgotten the printing press. William Caxton turned the first handle in 1477, and by the late sixteenth century vast numbers of books were being produced. Included in these were a growing number of pattern books, and these, rather than actual objects, had most effect on design in the seventeenth century. That is why frescoes, marquetry, metalwork, architecture and clay all use the same motifs, copied from the same source books.

Before the Restoration in 1660, English gardens were mostly old fashioned and modest. Since Henry VIII's time the nobility had incorporated Italian ideas into the grandest houses, but simpler mediaeval gardens were still common. In these we can presume the use of a few pots, very much along the lines of Gothic gardening, and pots would certainly be used in the "Italian" gardens.

When Charles II was in exile in France, he and his nobility had lived among the complex glories of Le Nôtre's gardens. These were even more formal and precise than the Italian gardens which had inspired them. On his return to England, he brought with him a craze for formal gardens in the French style, and all their many accessories.

These French-style gardens lacked the charm of their Italian models, imposing what I find is a deadening and over-rigid order, and an often vulgar use of grotesques and blocks of colour. I sense a hint of the same reaction from John Worlidge who, in his *Systema Horticultura or the Art of Gardening* published in 1683, describes the use of garden ornament by the Italians as a "vanity", and comments that this "mode of adorning gardens with curious workmanship is now become English".

That having been said, his Puritan inclinations are swept aside when he writes, "Other ancient Ornaments of a Garden are Flower-Pots, which *painted white* and placed on Pedestals, either on the ground or in a streight line on the edges of your walks, or on your walls, or at the corners of your squares, are exceeding pleasant."

A less restrained writer might have suggested a different colour of lime wash. When Celia Fiennes rode through England side-saddle in the last decade of the seventeenth century, she described a typical garden of the period at Durdans in Surrey: "Two middle walks run up to a double mount which cast the garden into three long grass walks which are also very broad, with three flower potts." There was also a maze, beside which was a large square pond "in nature of a canall" and flowerpots painted blue and red on raked gravel beds, no doubt extremely eye-catching in the manner of the times.

I have discovered that the large ornamental flowerpots demanded "to hold shrubs round a formal garden" often came from Holland, like much garden knowledge. George London and Henry Wise, in their *Retired Gardener* of 1706, state that "Pots must be either of plain earth or Dutch ware, the latter being much larger." It was not long before English potteries, often using foreign expertise, began trying to capture part of this market. One of Wise's apprentices, Stephen Switzer, was a prolific author and correspondent, and in the fourth edition of one of his pamphlets, entitled *A Compendious Method for the Raising of the Italian Broccoli, Spanish Cardoon, Celeriac, Finocchi, and other Foreign Kitchen Vegetables*, he sings the praises of

John Rose, the Royal Gardener, presents the first pineapple grown in England to Charles II. Behind the king is an urn painted brown with white swags in the manner of the day.

These "vasa's and urns" are shown in Switzer's pamphlet: Raising Italian Broccoli . . . , as, "Things which lend to the improvement of the ornamental Part of Gardening."

one Mr Aaron Mutchell, potter at Vauxhall (now part of London). As well as making drainpipes copying Roman models recently excavated in "Hide-Park", and "earthen tunnels for the cure of smoking chimneys" (which I take to be some of the first chimney pots), he makes "several sorts of Vasa's, Flower-pots and urns".

In fact these pots were almost certainly fired to a higher temperature than "plain earth" terracotta. They foreshadow the durability of "Coade stone", developed in the 1760's, which added ground glass to a white "ball" clay to give an extremely hard finish in pale stone colour. True terracotta, because of its porosity, is always vulnerable to frost if it is not meticulously prepared and fired, and much peasant or country pottery was neither. So Switzer eulogises Aaron Mutchell's wares as being "not so liable to be hurt by the frost", and adds that "if plac'd out of the reach of unlucky boys, they will undoubtedly last many years".

These experiments in imitating foreign models were short lived. The English Landscape Movement gave expression to the new awareness of Nature which was fostered by the poets and artists of the time, and was later reflected in the political philosophy of Jean Jacques Rousseau.

Soon all formality and geometry were swept

A mid-eighteenth century potters' workshop as shown in Diderot's Encyclopédie. The thrower kicks the flywheel at the beginning of a pot, while his apprentices roll out sausages of clay, coil the rim onto a square box and put the spouts onto a tulip pot or "cassette". Firewood is stacked next to the kiln in the background.

aside by Lancelot 'Capability' Brown, the great champion of the Movement, and armies of navvies were employed to raze the terraces so elaborately made a few decades before. With this new fashion, all "urns and vasa's" were banished to the vegetable garden and the potting shed.

But the humble flowerpot of "plain earth" had won itself a place in gardening that was to withstand the vagaries of fashion.

The English nurseryman and horticultural ware

With the growth of interest in gardening throughout the seventeenth century a new trade developed – that of supplying plants and accessories. As far back as 1515 John Chapman's great garden at Hampton Court had needed two large cart loads of "pottes for the erberes", costing one shilling and four pence to transport. These no doubt came direct from the potters, but by the late 1660s there were many florists and seedsmen, including well-known gardeners like Switzer, who sold seeds and sundries "at the sign of the Flower Pot over-against the Court of Common-Pleas in Westminster Hall", or Clements of Mile End, who in 1691 "kept a shop of seeds (and) plants in pots next the street".

Enthusiasm for gardening was reaching ever wider. The townsman is even considered a possible gardener when John Worlidge states that there is "scarce an ingenious citizen that by his confinement to a shop, being denied the priviledge of having a real garden, but hath his boxes, pots or

other receptacles for flowers, plants, etc."

Nurseries sprang up to meet the growing demand for plants. London and Wise founded theirs in 1681, at Brompton Park, near where the Kensington Museums now stand, and by 1705 they had a stock of ten million plants on well over 50 acres of land.

All this meant steady work for the potters making functional flowerpots, as opposed to the ornate urns for more decorative use. Common flowerpots are ideal for propagation and as a way of moving plants around, although sacking and baskets were also used for this. Another London nurseryman, Henry Woodman, writing to a northern client in 1729 and describing what he has had shipped, says that he "cou'd not have any small Baskets made for ye Cowcumbers. I fancy small potts will do as well which may eaisely be had at Newcastle."

The steady flow of new plants into England were all kept in pots. "Curious greens", that is to say exotic evergreens, were particularly sought after, especially oranges, oleanders, aloes, cacti, bays and myrtles. The numbers of pots used were sometimes enormous. Estate inventories of the

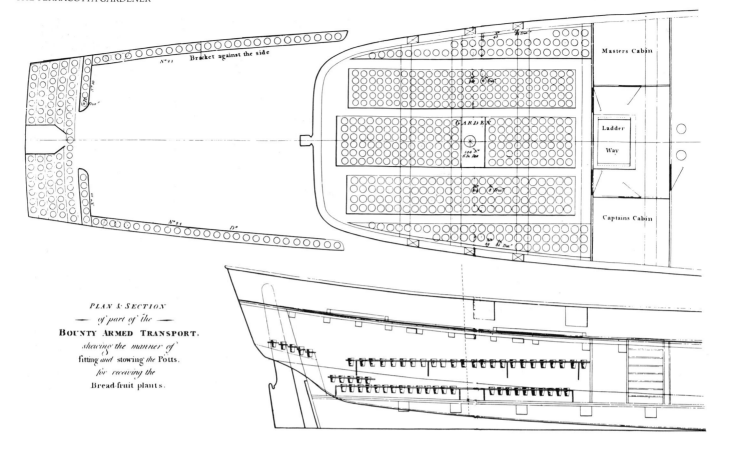

PLAN & SECTION
— of part of the —
BOUNTY ARMED TRANSPORT.
shewing the manner of
fitting and stowing the Pots,
for receiving the
Bread-fruit plants.

time often list hundreds of potted plants, and presumably only large specimens are mentioned. One household boasted nine thousand pots of asters alone.

By the mid-eighteenth century, English gardeners could call upon a wealth of nurserymen, with each generation adding knowledge and new discoveries. Horace Walpole states the norm in 1755 when he counsels a friend to buy "cypresses in pots at half a crown a piece; you turn them out of the pot with all their mould, and they never fail". In 1775 the first priced catalogues appear, offering transport by canal to extend the market.

Common horticultural flowerpots became ever more numerous and varied in shape. At the height of the Country Potteries' production in the mid-nineteenth century, the Victorian nurserymen could choose from a complicated but logical system of plain flowerpots which has never been equalled anywhere in the world. Not only was every size of plant catered for, but also different shapes of rootball.

Everyone is familiar with the basic flowerpot shape, although in Victorian times there were still many local variations, some taller and some squatter. This common shape was called a "full pot". Shorter in proportion than these were "half pots",

By the eighteenth century vast numbers of plain flowerpots were often used for transport. In the ill-fated Bounty, the space between the decks was adapted to carry breadfruit trees.

and shorter still were the shallow "seed pans". Taller than full pots were the delightful "long-toms", although these were never made bigger than about 9 inches in diameter due to their being easily knocked over and rather difficult to throw.

As for the various sizes of each type, that was governed by their "cast" number. A "cast" was in fact a unit of pay based on the weight of clay used. A single cast "full" pot weighs half a hundred-weight and will be over 21 inches in diameter.* A "halfcast" pot – two made to the cast – will be about 18 inches across, while a "60" – sixty made to the cast – will be 3½ inches across. A skilled thrower would make twenty cast a day, meaning twenty number ones or twelve-hundred 60's; each day's work being worth the same pay.

Full pots could be ordered in any of the following cast sizes: 1, 2, 4, 6, 8, 10, 12, 16, 24, small 32,

* These are the measurements I learnt when I trained at Wrecclesham in the Hampshire tradition. The Royal Horticultural Society's *Dictionary of Gardening* differs, but it used regularly to revise its own list of measurements, reflecting local variations, and no doubt there is a certain unwillingness by the potters to be too tied down!

Thomas Kent, as stated in his obituary above, was a "kind-hearted gardener" from the West of England.

Before the days of electric light, potteries were dark, mysterious places. Throwers always kept the window to their right, kicking the treadle with their left foot.

large 32, small 48, large 48, unrimmed 54, rimmed 54, unrimmed 60, rimmed 60, 72 and 90. Nineties, or "thumbs", were tiny 1-inch pots for tomato seedlings, and 72's, or "thimbles", were used for starting cauliflowers. All pots from 54's up were normally thrown with a thickened rim, the smaller ones without. Halfpots and seedpans always had rims, longtoms rarely.

It was commonplace for large nurseries to put in an annual order for half a million small pots, every one hand thrown.

A range of forcers was also developed for bringing on some early crops. The smallest were for indoor winter chicory, the middle size for seakale, and the largest, beautiful 2-foot-high bell-shaped cloches with a lidded opening at the top, for rhubarb.

An old head gardener once told me how they used to use these before the First World War in a grand garden near Henley-on-Thames. In late autumn, the rhubarb forcers were placed on the dormant crowns, though these should not have been forced for the previous two years or their vigour would suffer. Then two carters were set to work, the one to bring cartloads of fresh manure, the other newly swept leaves. Alternate layers of leaves and manure were heaped around the forcers until they were completely covered. In February, this heap would have changed to compost which was removed and restacked elsewhere, leaving the

forcers to be cropped. The heat from the rotting leaves and manure would have brought on fresh pale pink sticks of rhubarb, ready for picking.

All the pots I have mentioned so far would have been thrown on the wheel, keeping their price well down. The only hand-built horticultural ware was the range of square and rectangular seed or fern trays with flared sides. These were always popular because they wasted no space on the greenhouse benches.

The greenhouse is the last link in this story. In 1833, plate glass was invented, and although initially heavily taxed, it soon made greenhouses widely affordable. A few years earlier in 1824, J.C. Loudon had this to say in the introduction to his *The Green-House Companion*: "A flower in the open parterre, though beautiful and gay, has yet something less endearing, and is less capable of receiving especial regard, than a plant in a pot, which thus acquires a sort of locomotion; and becomes, as it were, thoroughly domesticated. After choice things were planted in pots, things rare would be planted in them; and from things rare to things rare, foreign and tender, the transition would be natural and easy. Tender rare plants in pots would be taken into the house for shelter, and set near the

The English Country Potters developed a comprehensive range of horticultural ware for Victorian head gardeners, which included seakale and rhubarb forcers like these.

window for light, and hence the origin of the Green-house."

The Victorian's mania for tender bedding plants soon led them to experiment with mixed plantings, giving an entirely new dimension to gardening in ornamental pots. Looking through their nursery-mens' catalogues I realize how few species we now use compared with the astounding profusion readily available then; and alas the same can be said of flowerpots.

The English Country Potteries

The potteries that made all those Victorian flower-pots were highly specialized. If you look at a Victorian teacup with its dainty handle and painted saucer and then hold an old flowerpot in your hand you will quickly see that they cannot have come from the same place.

But back in the sixteenth century, tableware and flowerpots did come from the same local potter. During the seventeenth century, however, the potteries in Staffordshire, London and Bristol began producing more sophisticated pots, includ-ing higher-fired stoneware and blue and white

"Delft" ware, both imitating Continental types. They exploited the growing urban and middle class markets by using "pot merchants", and caused many small local potteries to go out of business. The ones that survived turned to a new market, always locally based. They made cheaper, cruder pots mostly for preparing or preserving food, and also increasing numbers of flowerpots for nurseries and gardeners. Without the new demand for large numbers of flower pots, the Country Potteries could not have survived.

The eighteenth century saw this divide widen between the urban pottery centres and the Coun-try Potteries. In Stoke-on-Trent they developed the craft into an industry. They used "jiggers and jolleys" to "throw" pots mechanically, moulds to make fancy ware and machines for their clay production. Canal transport meant that most parts of the country were accessible to the industrial producers, so the country potters were left with

We engrave two FERN CASES of terra-cotta, manufactured under the "Watsonian Patent" for Messrs. F. & G. ROSHER, Queen's Road West, Chelsea. The first is a graceful object for the conservatory

or the drawing-room, the other is to show the applicability of the fern bricks in other ways; for the great merit of this most ingenious invention is, that it can be introduced into any conservatory,

walls, or adapted to any design. The shells for the ferns are made to slip in and out. This fern case undoubtedly surpasses all productions of the kind, with reference to either elegance or utility.

In Victorian times, many of the firms who produced architectural terracotta also made extraordinary "flowerpots".

only what was very cheap, or very large and heavy, for these things were harder to produce mechanically and difficult to transport.

Like in Italy, bricks, tiles and pipes were often added to the range of pancheons, milk pans, chamberpots, ham salters, bread crocks, jugs and pitchers, chick waterers, paint pots, candlesticks, bread ovens, chimney-pots and the ever-growing range of flowerpots and forcers.

The zenith of the Country Potteries was reached about 1850. The Stoke-on-Trent potteries continued to erode the country potters' market as their white earthenware became more efficiently produced, and thus cheaper, and worse still, the railways arrived. Beer, cheese and bread began to be produced centrally in factories, rather than in individual homes, so the beautiful range of large pots once used in the kitchen became less and less in demand.

The country potteries that survived turned increasingly to flowerpots and bricks. When Absalom Harris established his pottery in Wrecclesham in 1874, he specialized from the start in flowerpots. At a time when many other potteries were failing, he managed to build up a thriving family business which by the First World War employed twenty people. He, too, made a few bricks and some old-fashioned bread crocks, but he mainly supplied large runs of flowerpots to nurseries, together with a range of "garden vases", imitating in a pleasantly naive and simple style the highly ornate extravagances of the big Victorian terracotta works. His family also developed a range of "art ware", a strange combination of mediaeval and art nouveau glazeware, usually rich green or blue, and sold at London shops like Liberty.

The First World War caused many Country Potteries and brickworks to close. The young men went off to the war and either never returned or came back to better paid jobs. A few struggled on. The Harrises at Wrecclesham did well by supplying nurseries with enormous quantities of plain horticultural ware. But the Second World War sounded the death knell for most of the potteries, and after the war even Wrecclesham was unable to rebuild much of its business.

Finally, the machine edged its way into this last bastion of old English tradition. Although a machine for making flowerpots had been invented a century before in the USA, and had largely replaced hand throwing there by the turn of the century, it was not until the 1950s that these machines were imported to England.

The storeroom at Lamprey's Pottery, Banbury, Oxfordshire, at the turn of the century. Plain flowerpots are stacked at the back in "bundles" under their respective "cast" numbers, with saucers, small pedestal urns, jugs and wallpots above them.

By the time I arrived at Wrecclesham in 1974 it was a lone reminder of a vanished age. Survival was from hand to mouth, and as an apprentice I took home £13 a week. The buildings had been put up over the years by the potters themselves, and it was a miracle that some were still standing. The potters had made everything possible themselves, even extruding sections of terracotta window frame to hold the glass, rather than buy wood. Shelving was made from old floorboards, held up by hazel "shot pins", or shived sticks, pushed into holes drilled in lengths of whitewashed saplings, all cut from the local common.

In the old days, clay was "won" out the back of the pottery. It was soaked in a pit with sand before being dug out into a steam-powered pugmill, which mixed the hard clay with the soft clay to make it useable. As the clay was unrefined, lime was often a problem, leaving small white pock-marks in a fired pot. Sand was always added to the clay, rendering it stronger to work with and less prone to cracking. Terracotta clays shrink as they

dry, and if a pot is dried too fast or unevenly, it will split and be useless. Sand helps overcome this. Getting the sand was a good excuse for a rare day out with the family, and a picnic would be taken in the old cart to sandpits several miles away.

I trained with Reg Harris – affectionately known as "Young Reg" to set him apart from his father "Old Reg" – and his cousin Fred Whitbread. They were the fourth generation of Wrecclesham potters, Absalom having learnt his craft at Drotford Pottery in Hampshire. Reg's two sons now run the pottery, which still makes good flowerpots, in the old buildings which they are gradually restoring.

Although I now throw large pots, and so follow in Young Reg's footsteps, I learnt most from Fred who was a superb smallware thrower. I took over my wheel from a potter called Harry, when he retired that summer at the age of 83. He had spent

Two World Wars stole the able-bodied away from the County Potteries, and left only old men and young boys. They pose for a last photograph, loading a kiln that is half fallen down.

his life making mainly 60's, and one idle lunch hour I calculated that he must have made in excess of ten million pots in his life, all on a kickwheel. His last day at work he had made twelve cast, that is seven hundred and twenty pots. To throw even that many you need to make three pots a minute, and to make a full day's twelve hundred, this rate must occasionally creep up to nearly five a minute.

Yet watching Fred, I never felt he was hurrying. Repetition had allowed him to relax while meticulously following a routine so swift that the slightest variation would result in a ruined pot. Throwing should be like a dance, with a set routine of movements dovetailing into each other. All unnecessary detail has been ruthlessly cut away by generations of throwers. Both hands are used equally. While one hand is snatching a finished pot from the still-spinning wheelhead, the other is already moving to pull a new lump of clay from the mound behind the wheel: or while the right hand finishes the final flare to a rim, the left is collecting the wire that will cut the pot free.

Throwing harnesses the hand, the mind and the heart to a common purpose, which no doubt accounts for the strong Zen Buddhist association with pottery in Japan. It is an occupation that requires total commitment once begun; you cannot pause to reflect during the throwing of a pot, and I can remember trying out of curiosity to say my two-times table when throwing smallware and losing the thread after "2 x 3 is . . .". My mind was in my hands.

This is surely the heart of craftsmanship. By the mastering of a technique, honed by generations of craftsmen, the spirit is allowed direct access to the world through the hands, unfettered by the ego.

Whichford Pottery

When I first came to Whichford seven years ago, I can remember the thrill of anticipation as the road snaked steeply down through overgrown banks, and I saw the November-evening smoke rise from the village below. It is an idyllic place, set snug beneath a wooded hill, thrown in a great arc around the sloping green.

But there is no more cricket on the village green to while away the lazy summer afternoons, and one by one the shops and the school have all closed. Like so many English villages, because of the pretty façade we are in danger of becoming a desirable retirement zone or a collection of ideal weekend cottages.

This is a long-term problem with no easy solutions, but one way forward must be the creation of more local jobs. So I find it very heartening that in Whichford the pottery now

Wrecclesham Pottery, Farnham, Surrey, about 1930. The potters made the bricks, tiles and even clay window frames themselves. Two bottle kilns poke out of the kiln sheds, and to the right stand the honeycomb walls of a drying shed for bricks. A railway leads from the clay pits to the pug mill, that stands beyond the central rose window.

employs twenty local people of all ages, none of whom had previous experience in pottery. It also gives me enormous pleasure to be able to prove that the old ways of working a rural craft are, with a minimum of reinterpretation, still viable.

I have never been able to accept "the inevitable progress of the machine." In line with William Morris and C.R. Ashbee, I believe that machines should serve man, and not vice versa. I find our society's continued mania for replacing men with machines inexplicable. In the field of pottery, I am certain that it does not even make economic sense, and the spiritual and moral devastation caused by unemployment or the mindless servicing of technology are too lightly dismissed. I wish local farmers would try questioning the accepted wisdom of ever greater loans to purchase still more sophisticated machinery. We need experiments with labour-intensive schemes, where the creative use of capital helps revitalize society rather than demoralizing it. Agriculture is still potentially the biggest rural employer.

Wherever possible, I employ a person rather than a machine. We make so large a range of pots that it would cost hundreds of thousands of pounds to follow the modern way and begin "tooling up", and I prefer to invest instead in the skills of my labour force. Training becomes very important, because the quality of the pots reflects each individual's level of experience rather than the impersonal certainty of a machine. I encourage all who work with me to be their own critic, and to take responsibility for their own area of work. Newcomers sometimes find this lack of hierarchy baffling, but it forces everyone to be more aware, to think for themselves. It is very exciting to see a

team of skilled craftsmen and women work out a common approach to the challenges of their work.

There are seven throwers at Whichford, including apprentices, and the most skilled of us throw over half a ton of clay in a day. We work with the same techniques and at the same speed as the Victorians, and the "cast" system is still our yardstick, but these days we work shorter hours and take the occasional holiday!

We also make hand-pressed ware, which I learnt about in 1985 when I travelled to Impruneta on a Churchill Fellowship. The more ornate shapes and designs of these pieces make an excellent foil for the simpler, more direct forms of the thrown pots. Some floor and edging tiles and occasional brick "specials" help fill the gaps in the kilns, and we also produce a range of tin-glaze "Delft" tiles, hand painted on our own biscuit.

Absalom Harris would feel quite at home at Whichford. As in any country pottery, there is always plenty going on, with teams of people chatting and joking while they pass pots into the kiln, turn over rows of leather-hard ware, or stack the finished pots in the stockyard. The pottery is purpose-built, and looks like an old barn conver-

Whichford Pottery, Warwickshire in 1989. Although everything in the photograph is new, the pottery and surrounds are designed to feel like an old country workshop rather than a modern industrial unit.

sion from the outside, with an upstairs and downstairs. As at Wrecclesham, the throwing is all done upstairs, using the heat from the kilns below to dry out the pots.

We refine our own clay, using a combination of two local clays which arrive by the lorryload "as dug". The clay is first shovelled into wheelbarrows and tipped into a "blunger" (a 450-gallon mixing bowl with rotating blades inside), where it is mixed with water into a "slip". This is then passed through a sieve to remove impurities, and pumped under pressure into a "filter press". Our filter press weighs 14 tons, and is nearly one hundred years old. It traps the clay in sixty enormous metal "leaves" while allowing the water to be forced out. After a few hours of pumping slip, the press is gradually opened up, leaf by leaf, and the newly-formed cakes of clay are taken out and put in a "pugmill", which mixes the hard and soft parts together. We age our clay for a few weeks before a final "pugging". It is then ready to use.

The kilns at Whichford are the most radical modern change. We designed and built both of them ourselves using ceramic fibre, a super-insulator which looks like cotton wool. To make a kiln, 4 inches of it are hung inside a 7-foot square metal box, efficiently, although unromantically, replacing the massive piles of dusty bricks that made up the old kilns.

It still takes several days to "fire" large flower-pots. Even when apparently bone dry, clay holds water which will boil when heated up, and can blow the pot apart as it expands and changes to steam. So the early part of a firing is devoted to "steaming" the pots dry, and it takes at least twelve hours to reach 400°C (752°F). Thereafter, we increase our temperature at only 60°C (140°F) per hour to maintain even firing throughout the kiln. After twenty-six hours, the kiln reaches its top temperature of 1,000°C (1,832°F) when the pots glow a pale straw yellow.

The top temperature reached is very critical. If "underfired", the pots are not frostproof and are too porous, and if "overfired", they start to shrink dramatically and slump out of shape as they begin to melt. Pots "dunt" with hairline cracks if they are cooled too fast. If very big pots are being fired, we

The two pieces being joined together here were made the previous day, and so have stiffened slightly. When in place, the "bat" which the potters are holding is cut from the upper part. The pot is then thrown into its final shape and the decoration added.

The finishing touch.

leave the kiln to cool for three days.

There are many hazards in making pottery. Whole kilnloads can be overfired by forgetfulness. A window left open on a windy day can cause warping and cracking, poor clay preparation can lead to bad temper among the throwers. My work force need to be dedicated and self-motivated. It helps that most of us live in the same village, and many have known each other all their lives. It is a "family" business in the sense that two generations, or brothers and sisters, work together. As a result they are happy to give of their best, even when this includes rushing to the pottery late at night to "close a damper", or turn off a kiln.

I owe a great debt to the English Country Potteries for giving me the structure within which to develop my own ideas. Our working methods and designs stretch back into the past, but they also provide us with a viable framework for dealing with the complexities of the present.

An old terracotta oil jar, bought in an antique shop in Ascot, has turned white with age, allowing Mrs Merton to trail shocking pink Verbena 'Sissinghurst' down its lime-encrusted curves. (See page 136.)

DISPLAYS IN TERRACOTTA

I first remember terracotta in dusty "bundles" at the back of the old potting shed. Then I see it resplendent, shining in warm antique glory on a Florentine terrace. In between are endless personal interpretations and subtle uses. I have tried to recall some of these with the help of fourteen fine gardeners, who all share my enthusiasm for clay pots, grand or simple.

When I was choosing which gardeners I should invite to contribute to this book, I tried to strike a balance between the many styles and interests which make gardening so fascinating. There follows a lively juxtaposition of different uses and plantings of pots, which reflect the personalities of the gardeners. The settings range from small town gardens to traditional cottage gardens, manor houses and stately homes. In each case, my first priority was to like the garden myself. Many were already full of terracotta and I supplemented this by contributing pots I had collected; choosing shapes and sizes I felt complemented the garden.

I left the choice of planting entirely to the gardeners, and before writing each section, I spent an afternoon talking to each person about gardens, pots and life in general. I have banished precise technical information about each pot to the next chapter, except where it fits in with a more general appraisal.

At the end, I hope you will share my enthusiasm for all the hard work and inventive ideas offered here.

The lilies in this planting were suggested by the decoration on the pot, but the agave shooting over the rim shows Mrs Merton at her experimental best. (See page 136.)

THE OLD RECTORY
Pots to the Fore!

Mrs Merton

I have always been pot mad," laughed Mrs Merton. "I find that you can use pots to jazz up the garden. I do not like boring bits anywhere; everything must be floriferous. We have a long, bare terrace here, so I cover that with pots."

When the Mertons moved to the Old Rectory, Burghfield, in 1950, they created the garden from scratch. While her husband, Ralph, laid out the form of the garden, Mrs Merton began to acquire her now formidable knowledge of plants. Her Danish mother had been a keen gardener, but her exhortations to "Come along, Esther dear, deadhead the pansies or help weed the paths" put her off becoming an enthusiastic gardener until she was nearly forty.

"I never meant to be a horticulturist. I did not do botany or anything useful at school because it bored me. Now I never have my nose out of a book. I do find it a most rivetting, fascinating subject. The more you read, the deeper you go. Lovely."

Mrs Merton's passion for plants has taken her all over the world on collecting expeditions. "Our bathroom would always turn into a greenhouse, and I would be bunging the most dreadful bugs down the lavatory. I have some really wonderful things in those flower beds out there from China."

It is not only exotic strangers that capture Mrs Merton's heart. She loves cottage-garden flowers, extravagant roses, aromatic herbs, ferns, daturas, scented violas ... "Every single plant here has some meaning to it. One becomes awfully sentimental in gardening: Oh yes, that was my Granny's. A lot of that goes on."

Like a painter with a sophisticated range of colours to her palette, Mrs Merton's knowledge of plants is a rich resource for her imagination when she plans a planting. She works with her gardener, Susan Dickinson. "It all starts off in my head. I know what I want – usually the most extraordinary things that one cannot find. Then we group the plants together before planting out, and Susan says 'Do you like it like that?' and I say 'Yes!' or 'Ugh!' Often we carry plants around to get exactly the right shades of colour."

Susan loves working with Mrs Merton: "We colour scheme the plantings together, certain pots for certain colours. For example, the cordyline always goes in the 'red' pot, but we change the plants every year because we are always coming across new things that are fun to try out."

In recent years, a row of very large flowerpots has been installed along the terrace which separates the sitting room from the main garden. The size of these pots make them a real challenge to use, and each year the plantings become more daring, although they always follow the same basic rules. A tall centre acts as a core, with bushier plants of medium height around it. Trailing plants around the edge of the pot grow into a "skirt" to complete the composition.

These plantings are distinctively generous, and have the height and balance that
distinguish a good flower arrangement,
which is one thing with cut flowers and
branches, quite another with growing
plants.

Mrs Merton's garden has many delights,
but it is the stunning arrays in her large
pots that are becoming legendary.
Flowerpots give Mrs Merton a special
opportunity for the creative side of gardening that she really enjoys: "I first used
flowerpots when I lived in France. You
had to there *faute de mieux*, because it gets
so dry. I loved the range of possibilities
pots offered, and I still use them wherever
I can.

"It's a marvellous thing. You know, it
really is gardening of the future. Pots to
the fore!"

*Several years ago, Mrs Merton
changed the old 18-inch pots on
her terrace for larger 27-inch
pots. She and her gardener,
Susan Dickinson, have taken up
the challenge of these big pots
quite systematically. Every
planting is divided into three: a
core of tall plants; a surround of
lower "midriff" plants; and a
trailing "skirt" cascading to the
ground. Each pot is given a
colour scheme. Within this
framework, new ideas and
species are tried out every year.
(See page 136.)*

Although this pot is only 20 inches in diameter, it holds seventeen plants, of seven different species. Complementary colours are used here, zest being given by the great range of leaf shapes.(See page 136.)

Thinking of ideas specially for this book, Mrs Merton grouped these pots in a dark corner to give hope to those who may have despaired of their shady back gardens. Three months old, the plantings have become marvellously lush, with their pale greenish yellow foliage shining out of the gloom. This corner is so dark that the photograph had to be taken with a flash, even in daylight. (See page 137.)

Not every pot in Mrs Merton's garden is full .... This little Cretan jar sits by itself among pansies and ladies' mantle.

Beside the old conservatory is a little terrace, fondly known as the French garden. A high brick wall shelters a mass of pots brought out of their winter quarters for the summer. These two plantings are sited on the low wall at the front of the terrace.

The robust purples of Heliotropium Marine go surprisingly well with the deep orange of new terracotta in a curvaceous planting on the left. To its right, by contrast, a cordyline shoots out of a pedestal pot brimming with the pointy leaves and flowers of Fuchsia 'Tom West'. (See page 137.)

A cordyline is the central feature of Mrs Merton's "red" pot. It is assembled with a different combination of plants each year. This season, the small red flowers of Salvia fulgens are dotted among the thin spikes of the cordyline, while trailing pelargoniums and fuchsias add colour and weight lower down. This picture was taken early in the season; by autumn the pot will have almost disappeared under the foliage. Compare this with the planting on pages 40-41. In the foreground is the same "red" cordyline pot, but in a different year with a variation on the theme. (See page 137.)

Edwardian baskets still in use at Powis Castle: vivid fuchsias against the deep green of ancient yew hedges. (See page 138.)

POWIS CASTLE
Renaissance splendour

Jimmy Hancock

I knew about the splendid terracotta plantings of Powis Castle long before I eventually managed a trip to the Welsh borders early one September. As a craftsman, I was eager to see the pots themselves, which I had heard were old – how old? How were they made? As a gardener I wanted to know if they were planted today in the same way as they were fifty years ago. I knew I would be fascinated by this rare example of a seventeenth century "hanging garden" brought to new life in the latter half of the twentieth century.

The history of the terraced gardens is unclear. They may well have been started during the period 1695–1722 when the castle was occupied by the Earl of Rochford in the reign of William and Mary. Laid out on the hill below the red sandstone castle, they were probably inspired by the formal gardens of the Italian Renaissance, particularly the Villa d'Este.

The "lower garden" and the herbaceous borders were introduced by the fourth Countess of Powis, from the turn of this century, from whose time, I discovered, date the famous basketwork pots. Powis was left to the National Trust by her husband in 1952, and it was in 1972 that Jimmy Hancock, the present head gardener, took over: "The Trust made the garden the sort of standard it is today. By 1972, very little of the work had been carried out, which was a great challenge for me. In most cases, the Trust takes over gardens that are already great, like Hidcote or Sissinghurst, and then you try and carry on in a similar style of planting. Well, I don't think that necessarily works best in gardens, because they are always moving. And as we didn't have any precedent – we didn't have a Gertrude Jekyll or anybody like that associated with the garden – we were not always restoring, and could create our own.

"There is another point to bear in mind: this area was actually a quarry – the castle was mainly built of stone that was quarried here. This seems a formal area, but it isn't planned as regularly as one might think. All the terraces are different depths, and although they start at one width, they don't always finish at the same. There are a couple of places where the natural rock actually breaks out, making one of the special micro-climates this garden is so full of. We're blessed here with very fertile soil which makes for very good, strong growth – you only have to look at the size of the oak trees. It also enabled us to have the tallest tree in Britain in the parkland nearby for quite a long time." Strolling along the terraces, admiring border plants twice the size they would be in my Warwickshire garden, I saw exactly what he meant.

It is not clear exactly where the Powis baskets came from. Similar ones were produced in several Country potteries, and they all suffer from the same problem. Small pieces of the basketwork fall off as frost gets in between them and the wall of the pot. The twisted handles have invariably been knocked off, leaving only a mark on the rim to show where they once were. The Trust have commissioned several local potters to make replacements, and also had five tall vases made for the five niches on the top terrace directly under the castle.

Jimmy Hancock relishes his duty of planting out the many different flowerpots at Powis. Along the balustrades, in niches and at the end of flights of steps, terracotta pots overflowed with fuchsias, helichrysums, geraniums (pelargoniums) or diascias; each one planted to complement its setting. "The pots here used to be brought in every winter and the plantings kept from one year to the next. The first year I came, I thought we could do just as well by replanting with fresh cuttings every year. So that's what we do now. I love trying out new ideas. I'm very fond of the fuchsias which we're well known for, and we still use *Pelargonium* 'Mrs Kingsley' which was here when I came, but I like to experiment, and it's always the new ones I keep my eye on to see how they perform."

At Powis Castle, yew and box hedges, the pink of the Stuart brickwork or the mists of a distant view give the flowerpots ideal settings. Jimmy Hancock's plantings harmonize with them perfectly in colour and form. "I think shape and foliage are the most important things. They are everywhere in a garden, and in a pot they cannot be avoided."

To reach the woodland garden that lies across a valley from the main terraces, you must pass along an old yew walk. This curved bench sits in a niche at the far end, flanked by two pots on stone pillars. Their rich colour glows against the shady greens.

I particularly like this planting. From far off, you see the bold pattern of hosta leaves. Only as you approach do you realize that some are not hosta at all, but belong to a canna. Hanging beneath them, lobelia shines out like ephemeral jewels scattered in the air. (See page 138.) This is a new pot made by Gwen Heany who has given it extra flare balanced by a strong squat shape.

A datura makes an impressive centre in this planting, which uses many different leaf shapes and colours. Creeping Nierembergia repens make an unusual and delicate skirt around the top of the basket. (See page 138.)

The earliest examples of basket-work pots that I have seen illustrated are in early seventeenth-century pattern books, where French woodcuts show them being carried by nymphs. The figures may be Flora or Pomona, the Roman goddesses, who roamed the earth strewing flowers and fruit from their baskets. The sides of these pots always curve gracefully out, and they came in two different proportions – the taller one shown here and a shallower version.

Jimmy Hancock has always used many varieties of fuchsia. Here he combines them with grey wisps of Calocephalus brownii which spill through the decorative handles of the pot. (See page 138.)

Five o'clock on a midsummer morning, when the sun turns everything golden. Melianthus leaves spread above reds and greens, with double nasturtiums flowing over the pot. (See page 139.)

Three sandstone niches are cut into the old brick walls that hold back one of the terraces at Powis. These fall away steeply below the castle and are part of the original garden. Mike O'Brien made these tall, narrow pots especially for these niches.

Salvia guaranitica bursts from a clump of Pelargonium 'The Boat'. The eye is centred by the brilliant yellow stars of Bidens ferulifolia. (See page 139.)

This is one of a pair of pots which flank the entrance to the lower fountain garden. They look magnificent from afar, and draw visiters towards the next room of the garden. Fuchsia 'Joy Patmore' in the centre of the plantings holds up a riot of pink Diascia rigescens.
(See page 139.)

In another niche on the terraces flying sparks of lobelia shimmer in the cold first light of dawn. It is so sheltered on these terraces that the hanging Lotus berthelotii has burst into unexpected flame-red bloom.
(See page 139.)

*Purple sage against rosy terracotta; a detail of one of the pots in the kitchen garden (see overleaf)
shows the Salisburys' initials intertwined within a marquess' crown.*

HATFIELD HOUSE
A Jacobean restoration

The Marchioness of Salisbury

The first time I visited Hatfield House in Hertfordshire, the seventeenth century home of the Cecil family, was to deliver some large pots I had made specially for Lady Salisbury. We had discussed their design on my stand at the Chelsea Flower Show. They were to be classic lemon pots emblazoned with the Salisbury coat of arms. When I returned to see the plantings which her ladyship had done this season, I was delighted to find my pots lining the main path of her new potager, or kitchen garden. Used for herbs, their colour responded well to the grey-greens and purples of sages and thymes. Other pots contained small olive trees in memory of John Tradescant, the first gardener at Hatfield, who grew the olive, first introduced to Britain in 1570, the year of his birth.

The Tradescants, father and son, were responsible for the original plantings of the Italian-style pleasure gardens designed in 1607 for the first Earl of Salisbury by Mountain Jennings. A Frenchman, Salomon de Caus, was employed to build an elaborate water parterre to emulate the celebrated water gardens of Italy. Sadly, the eighteenth-century passion for landscape cleared all this splendour away. After years of neglect, the second Marquess was spurred on by a visit from Queen Victoria to re-make a formal terraced Italian garden and extend the courtyards to north and south.

Regrettably, the Jacobean designs have not survived, so Lady Salisbury has had to rely on her knowledge of garden history when making her beautiful restorations. The spirit of John Tradescant is most directly conjured up by the garden she has created in front of the old Tudor banqueting hall where Elizabeth I held her first council. An exquisite knot garden contains plants that would have been known to Tradescant himself, including many that he introduced to England. Around the fountain in the centre are terracotta pots of clove carnations – the Tudor gillyflower – surmounted by arched canes in the manner often seen in old prints.

Hatfield House would have had terracotta pots in the seventeenth century but they, together with almost all the garden statuary and ornament, were swept away with the removal of the formal gardens during the eighteenth century. Lady Salisbury has had to find a number of suitable stone replacements to fit the magnificence of the descending terraces of the East Gardens. Nearer to the warm red brick of the house itself, she has used both stone and terracotta containers. Small groups of flowerpots add an informal charm and a human scale to its imposing facades. Lady Salisbury says that she prefers to plant each pot with a single species only, the old way of doing it, and then groups pots together for contrast and effect.

It is a surprise to many visitors that these splendid gardens are all grown and tended without artificial sprays or fertilizers. Lady Salisbury anticipated the current interest in organic gardening by many years, and since she started her first garden at Cranborne Manor in Dorset in 1954, she has always avoided the use of artificial insecticides and fertilizers. David Beaumont, head gardener at Hatfield, emphasizes the importance of caring for the soil: "Get your soil right and your plants will grow." Great quantities of rotted compost and farmyard manure are dug into a new bed in preparation for planting, and are also applied as mulches in a three-year cycle with calcified seaweed to redress the pH balance. For pots he uses a loam-based potting compost, John Innes No. 3, and maintains that "Plants grow better in a clay pot than they do in a plastic pot". David Beaumont dreams of restoring the old walled vegetable gardens to their Victorian splendour, and of using them to produce high quality organic fruit and vegetables.

Lady Salisbury uses the past as a creative spur while masterminding radical changes. In the near future she has plans to re-design both the north and the south courtyards. Since their inception, the Hatfield gardens have been repeatedly altered to suit new tastes and fashions. Change is once again bringing them new life, and I am glad to see that terracotta has won itself a small part in their restored glory.

One of the latest ventures at Hatfield is the kitchen garden where vegetables are organically grown in raised beds. Large lemon pots, planted with herbs, have been placed at intervals along the main avenue to point up the overall compositon. (See page 139.)

A deliberately random array of terracotta pots dots the steps above the majestic terraces of the East Garden. In the style of their seventeenth-century setting, the plantings are single species, often of exotic evergreens, or "curious greens" as they would have been called. (See page 140.)

A detail of one of the pots of sweet-smelling clove carnations (see overleaf and page 140.) The idea comes from old manuscript illuminations which the Marchioness of Salisbury came across when she was involved in the setting up of the Museum of Garden History at Lambeth, London. A Hampshire potter was commissioned to copy the pots, and David Beaumont and his colleagues spent a few winter evenings weaving the basketry out of lobster-pot cane.

An oleander in a traditional pot evokes the Mediterranean.

An English knot garden lies in
the courtyard area of the Old
Palace at Hatfield, which ends in
the Great Hall where Queen,
Elizabeth I held her first council.
   Immaculate box hedging
encloses only plants that the
Queen would have known,
together with those introduced to
England by John Tradescant the
Elder, who worked at Hatfield.
This garden hardly restrains an
abundance of flowers and fruit
within the confines of its
intricate geometry, although it
was only laid out in 1980.

BEECH CROFT ROAD
A city garden

Mrs Anne Dexter

Mrs Dexter's home stands in a quiet red-brick Edwardian terrace; a typical Oxford town house with bay windows to the front, and the standard narrow strip of garden at the back. But, apart from the dimensions, there is nothing standard about Mrs Dexter's garden. As you walk through her sitting room towards the south-facing French windows, you are suddenly confronted by a lush hanging garden. No routine patch of lawn here, but an ordered jungle rising high on both sides, cascading down to a narrow, serpentine path. Standing there, it is hard to believe that the garden is only 75 feet long by 21 feet wide. It holds several hundred different species of plants, mostly rarities, beside the fifty different kinds of clematis that festoon the background trees.

Mrs Dexter started the garden thirty-five years ago. "There was nothing here at all but a few blades of green things sticking out, supposed to be grass, and a huge rowan tree." She laid the crazy paving for the terrace and path herself, and built up dry stone walls bit by bit to make raised beds on both sides of the path. The garden is roughly divided into three compartments: alpines, herbaceous and shrubs. At the far end there is a secret place full of shade-loving plants, ferns, fritillaries, trilliums, and their kind. She looks after all this herself; providing supports for climbers, pruning back shrubs and trees up to three times a year, training, feeding, watering – it goes on and on. "It's very leg-aching, sometimes," she admits.

And pots? There is certainly no room for huge urns here. "The pots are just the little twiddly bits finishing off the garden", she said. They are the first things you see coming into the garden, set on the sun-filled terrace at the back of the house. They are an ideal introduction to Mrs Dexter's garden, because they invite you to look in an intimate, small-scale way – to slow down, and explore in detail.

Rectangular terracotta troughs fill the windowsills and surround the steps. The child in me was delighted, gazing at these exquisite landscapes, with their succulents and alpines nestling like strange trees among outcrops of tufa.

Mrs Dexter inherited a lot of pots from her mother: "And no doubt her mother before her – they never seemed to break anything in those days." I found one seed pan with a particularly fancy roulette pattern run around it, and quite a collection of square pans and half pots. They were made in Cumbria, where the damp weather encouraged Mrs Dexter's mother to grow her succulents in pots. Her grandmother was also an enthusiastic gardener, creating a "Victorian garden with poles and roses and auriculas. And I remember the cool of the dairy, where terracotta pans of milk stood on slate shelves, and the cheeses were stored up on top." It is not only pots that Mrs Dexter inherited. Looking at her amazing garden, you feel as if the knowledge and love of plants of three generations has been condensed into this tiny city garden.

Mrs Dexter's alpine troughs are whole gardens in miniature. Each one contains many different species, beautifully arranged with tufa and gravel, like a Chinese landscape.

I made this pot for Mrs Dexter to replace one of her grandmother's that was broken. It is ideal for alpines, with steeply-sloping sides ending in six short legs which hold the pot up from the ground. It is made by pressing the clay into a mould which has details of the legs and rim already in it. (See page 140.)

This specimen *sempervivum* is kept in a small round seedpan with three legs to raise it off the ground. The flattened rim has been lightly crimped by pinching it between fingers and thumb, in the manner of old Devon slipware. (See page 140.)

Although only three years old, this rectangular trough has acquired a fine patina. Its simple shape is set off by a precisely crimped rim, where a sharp wooden tool has been pressed into the damp clay. (See page 141.)

A detail from an old Cumbrian seedpan which belonged to Mrs Dexter's grandmother. The chequered pattern is applied with a "roulette" just before a thrower removes the finished pot from the wheel. A roulette is made from a piece of clay, brass or wood the size of a cotton reel, with decoration carved into its side. It is put on the end of a small handle so that it can spin round freely. When pressed against the pot for one turn of the wheel it leaves an imprint of its decoration. The four deep grooves below the roulette marks were made by the tines of a tablefork.

*Mrs Connie Franks stands at her garden gate. She has lived in
the same cottage all her life. It is set in a delightful, and unruly,
patchwork of flowers, shrubs and narrow paths.*

SOUTHSIDE
Higgle-piggle garden

Mrs Connie Franks

I arrived at Connie Franks' delight-ful cottage garden in torrential rain. I had asked for directions on the way through the Oxfordshire village. "Mrs Franks' house? Oh yes, the one with the lovely garden." For all its efforts, the rain could not spoil the brave show of flowers and vegetables, densely packed all over the garden. Plants filled every corner, bursting out of the beds which surround the cottage with hardly a pause for the occasional path.

The vigour of the garden was matched in every way by its maker. Mrs Connie Franks has lived in her cottage in Steeple Aston for the last seventy-five years, and she is full of anecdotes about her garden and village, all told with a fine Oxfordshire turn of phrase.

As we sat drying-out over a cup of coffee, I asked her how she would describe her garden. "Well now, it's an old-fashioned cottage garden. You can't knock into some peoples' wooden heads the difference between a cottage garden and these gardens that are all laid out in rows and borders and patches. That wouldn't do in a cottage, not by any means," she said emphatically. "A cottage garden is tidy, but it's higgle-piggle. Nothing in squares or rows; it's just dug about. Like that," she pointed outside. "That's a 40 yard frontage, and that's all grown. It's all dug, it's all planted. Yes, that's a real cottage garden."

Connie Franks started her garden about forty years ago, when the cottage garden was still a familiar sight. She reckons her success is due to a combination of good sense, experience, and being willing to try things out to see if they will work. She also has the benefit of her family background: "You see, my parents, my grandparents and all my brothers were in the gardening line. They all worked in beautiful gardens like Luton Hoo. I remember the seed catalogues, which came in December in the days when I was a child. They were as good as a Christmas book to me, you know, because I was fascinated by all the flowers."

The wide variety of plants in Mrs Franks garden is often helped by chance as well as by choice. "There's no end of things that have seeded in there that I've never planted. If I don't like it, I yank it out when it's flowered; but if I like it, I leave it.

"That fuchsia there, I found under a seat on the bus. No one knew whose it was, so the driver let me have it. Nearly all the roses are from cuttings I've taken of my own plants. You start off years ago, buying a plant from Woolworths – like a 'Queen Elizabeth' pink rose for two shillings and four pence – and from there you take cuttings, and you can have as many as you like. It is as simple as ABC. I'm always getting cuttings from other people, too, and then I don't say, 'That's a something', I say, 'That's a Mrs Somebody'."

The rain had stopped at last so we went outside. We were faced by a mass of begonias and pelargoniums, all set in pots at the edge of a rough, wide path: reds, yellows and a flame colour of which Mrs Franks is particularly fond. "That begonia there is over thirty years old. Multiflora Flamboyant is the name, and I got it from Parkers of Manchester, one and sixpence a corm."

Among her pots, I spotted a square trough, made by Sankey and Sons. "Everybody falls in love with that pot. I've had it about sixty years, and it was old when I got it." As well as flowerpots, Mrs Franks uses anything else that will hold flowers, including chimney pots, a colander and a "sidlip", once used for sowing corn.

People often ask her how she finds the time to plant and look after her garden. "Well now, I don't do anything but tidy it up. Once it's planted, that's fixed, permanent." She admits that it takes her two hours to water everything, and that a garden is a lot of work.

She has little time for the busy lifestyle of the new car-driving, commuting villager: "How many people really like working a garden now? Not very many. They think it's fun, but all they really need in the long run is one about the size of a couple of flowerpots. No, no, they'd dance all day on sixpence, and you'd never know where they'd been. I remember when men used to catch the six o'clock morning train from Heyford to go to the steel works at Cowley, and didn't come back till late. But they all had allotments, they could grow stuff, any amount of it. They could show in the flower shows. How did *they* manage to find the time?"

Perhaps she has the answer. Looking wryly around at her tiny cottage she mused: "You see, if you have a contented mind, it's amazing where you can stay, isn't it?"

These two pots greet you by Mrs Franks' iron front gate. The "herb" barrel, made by Mark Griffiths, stands on an upturned seedpan to give the nemesia a chance to trail. Later in the season, the plants will be a great ball of orange, yellow and red, with the pot almost invisible. On the bank, a pan with handles, made by Jonathan Garrett, shows signs of the wood flame used in the kiln where it is "flashed" grey. Behind the "herb" pot, Mrs Franks has used a piece of hollow tree trunk as a container. (See page 141.)

Beside the front path, Mrs Franks fields a great array of pots, all holding extra summer colour. Geraniums grow in a wavy-edged bowl. This rests in the top of a Victorian hand-pressed chimney pot, filled with stones and earth. The picture is completed with an informal arch of clematis and rose. (See page 142.)

Old brick paths have all the warmth of terracotta, They were laid in soft earth or sand, sinking where most people walked. Moss grows in the cracks and they wear smooth with use. Mrs Franks' paths have a pleasantly uncertain edge, and the garden often intrudes onto the path. The pot here links the two, bringing the plants towards the centre of the path. (See page 142.)

This old square pot was made by Sankeys, a Midlands firm who were one of the biggest hand-makers of flowerpots in this century. This one would have been pressed by hand in a mould, and would be used for ferns or raising seedlings, the square shape taking up less bench space than a round pot. Mrs Franks loves begonias, and has kept some of these corms for over thirty years. (See page 142.)

A potted duck floats on a sea of gravel. Even its eggs are there.(See page 143.)

WOODROYD
Pure escapism

Alan Titchmarsh

When Alan Titchmarsh and his wife arrived in Hampshire in 1982, one of the first things they did was to build dormer windows into their house so that they could survey the garden from above. It was not an encouraging sight – a neglected north-facing slope, made up of clay, flint and chalk.

Luckily, Alan has a good sense of humour and plenty of energy to back up his gardening skills, and seven years later you would never guess the struggles that have gone into making the garden.

He used sticks to mark the positions of the trees, and then drew in lines for the paths and beds, Alan first ensured that the garden had good "bones". Inside these, he went on to create a series of smaller areas, each of special interest and variety. His greatest joy is juggling combinations of plants to create changing displays of colour and form.

Terracotta gives him a good opportunity for composition of this kind. He also uses it for ornamental features and focal points. Alan is a great afficionado of terracotta, and early in his career he established his own particular relationship with it. I leave him to expand:

"My first meaningful encounter with terracotta pots took place one warm day in August 1964. At the age of sweet fifteen, I'd been taken on as a raw but enthusiastic apprentice gardener by the local Parks Department in Ilkley, Yorkshire. Ahead of me, five years of concentrated learning; but today, eight hours of washing pots.

Scraping algae and white encrustations from 3-inch clay flowerpots with the aid of a brush suffering from creeping alopecia and a tank of cold and muddy water is no way to forge a lifelong love affair. But love 'em I did, and my spaniel-like devotion to them continues.

"There were times when I was driven to distraction by them – cheap but hefty Spanish versions that crack in the first frost of winter – and times when sheer boredom led me to even smash a few (I contrived to fall up a flight of stone steps with yet another armful of dirty ones, that day in August, so I'd have fewer to wash). But plastic pots? Nope. They belong outside petrol stations, along with the plastic grass that covers the forecourt.

"My own garden is pure escapism. After twenty-odd years of professional gardening I'm seldom affected by the criticisms of gardeners of the 'tidying' school. No; my garden is *not* a wilderness, euphemistically known as a 'conservation area'; it has strong lines, but the beds and borders within those lines are filled to over-flowing with plant jungles.

"I'm not simply a plant-collecting plantsman. My greatest (and often most frustrating) gardening pleasure is positioning plants so that they not only look good themselves, but also show their neighbours off to good effect. I like views and vistas and surprises round corners, and novelties that will amuse visitors and make them giggle.

"Ornamentation is vital. It's a shame

that gardeners with bank balances of three figures rather than four have little choice when it comes to statuary. Sotheby's will offer you grandeur for thousands. Your local nursery will offer you a precast gnome or a damsel in deep distress (due, no doubt, to her flimsy drapes and the severity of English winters) for a handful of pounds. But the middle ground is occupied only by reconstituted stone replicas of classical figures, wellheads, columns and gatepost finials. Which is why I'm a fan of terracotta.

"Here is skill, artistry and fineness of form at an affordable price. I can position pots on steps, on my patio, underneath my arches, in and among my border plants. I can move them at will to change the scene, and I can replant them for a different effect whenever I'm bored, which I often am, and often do.

"Strange, isn't it, that although fashionable gardening writers scream about the hideousness of French marigolds and many other bright orange flowers, they *never* complain about the orangeness of terracotta. And it really *is* orange. It ought to clash with magenta and pink and heaven-knows what. But when did you last read that you shouldn't put a fuchsia in a clay pot because the two will scream at one another? You didn't. Somehow, we don't seem to notice.

"I'm glad my scrubbing days didn't put me off. If they had, I'd be stuck with a frozen damsel by now!"

Surely a desert island for some garden castaway? A lone "palm" (an aeonium) for shade, houseleeks for sustenance.... Alan Titchmarsh's plantings have a delightful humour to them, executed with an adroit hand. Here, Alan has covered the surface of the potting medium with coarse grit, both for its visual effect and as a mulch to sharpen drainage and prevent weeds. (See page 143.)

Master of the unexpected, Alan Titchmarsh combines a central ornamental cabbage with a frill of busy lizzy, using a small pedestal pot. It is an unprejudiced imagination that conjures up such a pairing, and the result is decorative as well as entertaining. (See page 143.)

East meets West. Pebbles and a Japanese maple evoke the orient, while the acanthus leaves and swags of the pot speak of a European heritage. Specimen trees can be successfully grown in a large pot or tub. This pair can stay together many years if the rootball is cut back slightly and teased free of old soil every autumn. (See page 143.)

This group of pots enlivens a bare corner of the terrace. The smaller ones introduce a sense of scale to the composition. Their detailed decorations emphasize the plain form of the Ali Baba jar which stands behind them, half hidden under a cascade of Helichrysum petiolare 'Aureum'. (See page 143.)

The pillared loggia at Tintinhull House is the perfect setting for the "jumble" of pots that Penelope Hobhouse brought with her when she arrived as curator for the National Trust. An upturned seakale forcer on the left gives ample root space for a large Bidens polyepsis. In winter the pots are put inside, and the loggia covered in plastic to give some protection from the frost. (See page 144.)

TINTINHULL HOUSE
Creative custodianship

Penelope Hobhouse

I find Penelope Hobhouse's books about gardens a delight, both for the writing and the generous illustrations, so I was looking forward to hearing her talk about her pots at Tintinhull, the National Trust property in Somerset in which she and her husband live. Tintinhull House itself is charming with its low Queen Anne front of mellow stone, but it is the garden which enjoys most renown. Laid out at the turn of the century in a series of formal courts or garden "rooms", it was extended and brought to life by the beautiful plantings of Phyllis Reiss, who moved there with her husband in 1933.

We sat and talked in Penelope Hobhouse's study surrounded by gardening tomes, situated, I noted, as far away as one could be from the alluring prospect of the garden. She is a dedicated gardener, an enthusiasm which was first triggered by visiting Tintinhull in 1956: "I was absolutely bowled over. Suddenly I knew that gardening was something quite wonderful. I count myself very, very lucky to now be responsible for its care and continuation.

"Because of the restrictions of Mrs Reiss's colour schemes I do get particular pleasure from choosing plants for the pots. Watering, tending and feeding the pots almost breaks us, and sometimes it seems tempting to give them up, but all in all we do love them and find it fun."

Before coming to Tintinhull as the National Trust curator, Penelope Hobhouse created a garden at Hadspen, about twenty miles away. "That was a garden completely different from here. I grew trees, shrubs and ground cover. I really did not think about colour schemes or anything, but I did grow a huge number of plants in pots. We had a sort of verandah by the house and I always loved doing that. Also, I have a passion for Australasian plants, which you mostly cannot grow outside in winter. I like making a jumble of pots, just as I like making a jumble in the flower bed. That's always been my sort of gardening.

"I came to Tintinhull nine years ago, and at first felt quite tentative about making any changes, about bringing in my own sort of gardening. It is just that we had promised to keep it as Mrs Reiss left it, so when I popped in something that wasn't on the list I would feel guilty. Luckily for me, I knew her, and came here while she was still alive, so I feel pretty confident that anything we do is what she would like. I believe that if Mrs Reiss was alive today, she would go mad about all these new things we can get — when she was gardening it was very difficult to find new exciting plants. At Sissinghurst, the attitude is that Vita Sackville-West was an experimenter, and so she would like her successors to experiment. We have taken that approach here too, rightly or wrongly. I really think that Mrs Reiss would only be amused by it, and pleased. We are just doing the best we can because we want the gardens to be beautiful."

It is known that Mrs Reiss installed the four large tubs which stand at the corners of the rectangular pool she built. When the National Trust took over, Graham Stuart Thomas introduced some pretty plantings of pelargoniums with trailing variegated ivy. But one year, when the soil was being replaced in the pots the ivy was left out and died. It was a mistake, but "we realized we had got rather bored of endlessly cutting off dead bits of ivy, so we thought we wouldn't do it for a while".

Today the poolside pots are magnificent. Planted with an unusual *Hibiscus trionum*, they frame the pillared loggia that stands at one end of the pool. This little summerhouse, full of comfortably battered wicker chairs, overflows with a lovely "jumble" of plants in an enormous variety of pots. It is clear that an enthusiast has accumulated these, now filled with special tender plants or carefully assembled colourful mixtures.

As you walk through the different "rooms" of the garden, you become aware of how pots are being used to soften an edge here or bring casual liveliness to a doorway there. They do not draw attention away from the overall effect but unobtrusively enhance the pleasing proportions of their settings.

"I believe that a garden like Tintinhull, which is a very formal garden (it looks awful if you have a single magnolia leaf on the lawn) has to be humanized by having odd, slightly eccentric things. I hope the next curator will collect primulas or something unusual. I think that gives a garden an edge. I happen to enjoy plants in pots. As most of the pots are ours, when we leave here they will all disappear, and what follows will be up to the new people."

Penelope Hobhouse was one of the first gardeners to experiment with lush mixed plantings in pots. This interest has led her to use many unusual tender plants. As she says,"I happen to enjoy pots", and this is one of the enthusiasms that she brings to the beautiful gardens at Tintinhull House. (See page 144.)

This illustrates some of the colours of terracotta, from pale orange through pink to white.

The square seed pan in the foreground is very unusual. It was thrown round on the wheel, and then pinched and beaten into a square at its rim. This is a clever and cheap solution to the perennial demand for square seedpans.

Silvery foliage overflows a Whichford-made swagged pot. On this, the decoration is integral. After throwing, the clay is allowed to stiffen slightly, and the wall of the pot is then pushed into a small plaster mould offered up to the outside. Although this leaves a dent on the inside, it means that there is no danger of a piece of decoration falling off in the frost.

*Ivy twists among chunks of stone, making a landscape in miniature. The lion closely follows a mediaeval
pattern made from gilded wood I found guarding the entrance to the old priory.*

BOURTON HOUSE
Terracotta collection

Mr and Mrs Paice

I challenge anyone who visits this Gloucestershire garden to find a single plastic pot. Even in the greenhouse, cuttings and stock plants are all in terracotta, and in the pot store "bundles" of clays lie cleaned and stacked, ready for the autumn migration back into the greenhouse.

There are exotic plantings all round the garden. In the courtyard, a cluster of terracotta is almost invisible under a jungle of plants. Another group makes a focal point where two paths meet. A stone sink spills over with unusual plants, and a vast lead cistern contains abutilons, fuchsias and geraniums on a scale to match. There are more than one hundred and twenty containers of one kind or another, all planted up quite differently.

Mr and Mrs Paice dislike plastic and simply will not use it, and that principle governs their choice of containers. "We like other natural materials as well, such as stone or lead, but it happens that terracotta has often been easier to find."

Their love of terracotta started in Spain, where they have a house near Barcelona. Over the years, they have witnessed the gradual death of the local potteries, and now the pots you could have bought in any local market two decades ago have become collectors items.

Mr Paice first tracked me down in 1980, when my pottery was still at Middle Barton, near Woodstock in Oxfordshire. He bought pots for the roof garden of his London office. When they acquired a country house with a large garden, their terracotta collection soon increased dramatically.

The improvements to Bourton House and its gardens show a keen eye for good design and everything, including the terracotta, is chosen with care: "Look at the architectural shape of a pot. These rhubarb forcers, for example, stand well on their own and do not need any addition. Size is very important. Potters often seem to make things that are too small, so a lot of what is available today does not have enough bravura. In many gardens all you need is one really terrific pot, and to plant it like mad. The practical advantages are that you can water a big pot half as much as a small one because you have got twice the amount of soil, and you can be much more adventurous about what you put in."

In 1983 began the slow process of restoring the house, which had had eight owners since 1953, each eager to leave their own stamp on the seventeenth-century interior. And the garden? "We knew nothing, absolutely nothing. Would you believe, we came here and thought that we could handle it all ourselves with a little weekend gardening." Realizing their mistake, in 1985 they employed Paul Williams, and he now has an assistant, although "we still need about twenty-five more people."

Talking to Paul Williams, he remembers that "we first started doing pots because there was nothing else in the garden. No plant interest, really nothing at all. So the first year we bought a load of geraniums and fuchsias from the Women's Institute stall in the market, and planted pots just to cheer the place up. Next we started heating the greenhouse and increased the range of plants, and we have had more and more fun as time goes on. In the same way, we have cleared out and redesigned the borders bit by bit. Mrs Paice and I work out the overall design of the gardens, but the planting ideas are mine."

I asked him how he approached planting up a pot: "It is the same as painting. You are using colours, textures and form. But with a picture you get it down and it stays there, whereas with these pots it's always changing and you have to redo it every year. I don't want to sound too arty-farty about it, but over the years you get to know what each plant is going to do, what you want the pot to look like, and how big it is all going to grow.

"I like to think it is all very light, and that there is a sense of humour in it somewhere. If you start taking yourself too seriously about all these things, you are going the wrong way, aren't you?"

This wallpot hangs to the right of the doorway through to the gardens shown on page 89. It is made by an Irish potter, Tony Murphy, working within the Devon slipware tradition. It is a darker red than most terracotta because it has been fired at a higher temperature to melt the glaze. (See page 145.)

At first terracotta was used to enliven a neglected garden. Now, sophisticated displays act as focal points in the new schemes created by Paul Williams. Here is one seen from the side, a chimney pot revealed behind a mass of yellow and red flowers. (See page 145.)

Putting several pots together creates a moist microclimate.
This helps prevent the plants drying out, and encourages them to thrive. (See page 145.)

Old rhubarb and seakale forcers, appreciated for the sculptural simplicity and strength of their forms, line the walls beside the greenhouses at Bourton House.

Away from the main gardens is a less formal area. An ever-changing display of pots cluster around the old pigsties where lop-eared rabbits and feather-footed bantams now live. Once past their peak, pots are put back in the greenhouse. or relegated to a supporting role, and new stars are brought on to take their place. (See page 145.)

The black foliage of ophiopogon is paired with a purple begonia, while the metallic spikes of a phormium are central to the larger planting. Set beside a new border with which they are connected by colour, features like these give interest and substance to a garden while the permanent planting gets going.

Paul Williams used his favourite kind of broad, nearly straight-sided pot, which gives a good depth of soil right up to the edge of the pot. (See page 146.)

This photograph, taken not long after the pots were planted up, shows how Paul Williams likes to group tall pots with smaller ones at their feet. By the end of the summer, the plants will have grown to cover the containers, creating a single homogenous mass of lush vegetation. (See page 146.)

Old nurserymen sometimes felt that a hole in the bottom clogged up too easily, so here the drainage hole is on the side.

A terracotta basket sits beneath an old stone urn. (See page 146.)

BARNSLEY HOUSE
Historical innovation

Rosemary Verey

Rosemary's books and her own garden at Barnsley House, Gloucestershire, have been the inspiration for a whole generation of gardeners. Her potager was almost the first indication of a new interest in decorative vegetable gardens, and it remains one of the most successful. You can find almost everything at Barnsley, pleached lime avenue, an old-fashioned herb garden, a tiny knot garden, and also an abundance of terracotta.

It can be busy at Barnsley, particularly since the garden won Christie's HHA Garden of the Year award in 1988, and between the bustle of the entrance and the quiet of Rosemary's study is a long courtyard brimming with plants in pots. Some of the larger flowerpots contain a mixture of plants with climbers and shrubs to give height, while others are kept deliberately low to be viewed from above. Plainer pots are planted with a single variety of lily or geranium. A seed pan with an ornate fern leaf pattern on its side spills over with houseleeks. A sweetly rounded pot made by David Garland is full of pinks surrounded with cane hoops in the Elizabethan style.

The plants are carefully chosen in response to their container; for example, the outward curving bell of a fuchsia bloom mirrors the curve of the pot beneath, and the bulbous forms of a "four-in-one" are comically challenged by the extravagant roundels of a large succulent.

Rosemary Verey loves the versatility of pots: "The beauty of it is that you can move them around wherever you wish, whereas if you have plants in the border you have to leave them where they are. It's also rather nice having them at different levels, isn't it? If you've only got a small space like a terrace garden, you can really go to town with pots."

Entering the house from the courtyard, it feels as if the garden has taken over inside as well as outside; the pots continue through the conservatory/dining room and the walls are clothed in green leaves. The library is full of gardening books. Rosemary Verey is an academic as well as a practising gardener and many of her ideas derive from historical models. For instance, her potager follows ideas found in William Lawson's *Country Housewife's Garden* of 1618 and the pattern for the knot garden was taken from Stephen Blake's *The Compleat Gardener's Practice* of 1664.

Along with her sense of history goes invention, the key to Rosemary Verey's gardening style. Her books and garden are packed with ideas, always stimulating her readers and visitors. Certainly, when we met for our interview, she was keener on a bit of innovation – namely, finding a good place for the 5-foot-high Cretan pot I had lent her – than on talking about past achievements. Off we sped to the potager where she suggested putting the Ali Baba right in the middle, a spot currently occupied by a fruit tree. "No, no," I said, slightly shocked, "you can't dig up a *tree*." Onwards to inspect vistas and backdrops, until we agreed on an informal setting beside a winding path.

A windfall find of a large number of old Ward pots "from a secret source" has given her more scope for terracotta; pots of herbs at the kitchen door, geraniums up the back steps, and ornamental box shapes hidden behind the stables to be brought out for the next local festivity. In spring, pots hold bulbs and scented violas, which in summer are replaced by pleasing combinations of tender perennials, half-hardy annuals and pretty foliage plants.

We went on to admire the Gothick-style pots that stand on the castellated terrace behind the knot garden. I unwisely hazarded a guess as to their origin to be met with humorous indignation: "Hampshire! I wouldn't buy anything from Hampshire. They came from Montepulciano in Tuscany. We must have brought them back in the early '60s. Everybody said they would split in the frost, but of course they did not. They are too good."

Although Barnsley House was built in 1697, I always notice the later embellishments. There is a Gothick summerhouse, a castellated verandah, a Doric temple - they are all full of pots. These Fuchsia 'Chequerboard' are grown as standards, and are carried indoors for winter. (See page 147.)

Enormous Cretan jars like these were first made by the Minoans four thousand years ago. They are still made in the same way today, though now they are more used in gardens than to store olive oil or wine.

This old seedpan is particularly shallow. It is, nevertheless, ideal for saxifrages. They survive outside in most weathers, and over several years naturally form a silvery mound.

A delicate summer planting, photographed early in the season before it fills out, stands in the corner of a sheltered courtyard. The new terracotta has been instantly "aged" by painting it with a mixture of old comfrey leaves and water.(See page 147.)

An ebullient echeveria with glaucous foliage fills a "four-in-one" pot. It was Rosemary Verey who first urged me to make these "four-in-ones" by showing me an old Italian one that was in her possession. They are made by placing three freshly-made pots in a triangle with a fourth one balanced on top, and "luting" them all together. (See page 147.)

A box tree sits on the terrace in an Italian Gothick pot. Complicated terracotta designs like this have usually survived from the second half of the nineteenth century, when there was a craze for all historical motifs, from Egyptian to High Gothic. (See page 147.)

Both these pots are thrown on the wheel. The larger one was made by Clive Bowen, a Devon potter. The decoration is lightly scratched into the damp clay and the handles are added last. The distinctive striations of the smaller pot are made by pressing the tips of the fingers into the finished pot while it is still spinning on the thrower's wheel. It comes from Crete. (See page 147.)

This venerable piece was given to Rosemary Verey by an impoverished visitor, in return for his fare to London. It is embellished with three thrown feet and a pattern of fern leaves, and the rim suggests that it might once have had a lid.

This is a small longtom, a type of pot developed for Victorian nurserymen to hold long-rooted plants. Taller than they are wide, their elegant looks are often short-lived when they blow over in the wind.

A circle of pots on a marble table; the two on the left with the white patina are made by David Garland, a painter and potter. Rosemary Verey has woven twigs to support the dianthus planted in this round bowl, a Mediaeval touch showing her love of garden history.
(See page 147.)

SUNNYSIDE FARM
Potter's choice

Jim Keeling

I cannot claim to be a very expert gardener, but I have always been involved in growing things. When I was six, I had a little garden down on the edge of the wood, overhung by old oak trees. The tiny cypress tree I planted now covers everything that was garden, and the battered concrete gnome who used to fish in his little pond must be buried somewhere underneath. I used to love filling up the pool, excavating paths or making a new rockery.

I am not much different now, and am forever starting some project or other in the garden. Last year it was mud walls. The drive to the pottery used to pass right outside the back door of my house, so with the aid of a mechanical digger we pushed the drive 20 yards into the field and constructed in its stead two gardens, both enclosed by mud walls capped with old tile roofs. Despite the incredulity of my workforce and all onlookers, these walls, 18 inches thick and up to 8 feet high, are now a permanent feature.

Mud was once widely used in England to make walls, even of houses, and if given good "hats and boots" will last for centuries. Our "mud" was made out of waste clay, sand, straw and a touch of lime. We built the walls up by hand, so they have a pleasant irregularity, curving this way and that, and even include a low, arched doorway.

Inside the main garden there is a central raised fountain overlooked by a tiled octagonal summerhouse with mud thrones inside, and a hearth for chilly May evenings. Geometric paths divide beds planted for me by Rupert Golby (page 123) with a riot of pinks, blues and whites and many scented flowers. After only a year it already looks very well.

My other pride and joy is the vegetable garden. This has old stone walls round it and has been in use for over 400 years. The soil is deep and black, and with its help I usually make a passable showing at the local Flower Show!

Then, of course, there are all those flowerpots. They do seem to get everywhere, and I am constantly changing them round to get a better arrangement or give a new focus of attention. I have always massed pots together, often standing larger ones at the back on piles of bricks or upturned pots, and recently I have taken to including stones and empty pots to make more complicated pictures.

My plantings are most often single species, and usually perennials, although I am learning a lot from this book! I love ferns, and have about twenty good specimens in 12-inch and 15-inch pots. Hostas are another excellent foliage pot plant, and I have kept a number of specimen trees alive in pots for many years – an *Acer japonica*, medlar, laburnum and *Salix helvetica*, a silver-leaved standard willow.

I have just started in 15-inch pots a few yew trees, which I am going to clip into various topiary animals, and I already have a lot of clipped box cones and balls of various sizes and two large bay pyramids.

The doorway of an old pigsty, with its complement of nettles and rosebay willow herb, was transformed by sliding in this oblong trough. (See page 148.)

I always plant up plenty of very small pots and seedpans, often with succulents or box balls, and put them around the base of larger pots. This emphasizes the scale of the big pieces and gives a family feeling, like Russian dolls.

With all these rich greens and strong foliage, backed up by a great array in shape and size of pots, I use very few flowers. When I do use them, I like them to be bright so that they shine out among the ferns or hostas; felicias, pelargoniums or nicotiana. Planting like this is not difficult, and I get enormous pleasure from the pots themselves, watching their different characters jostle for attention.

Outside my back door there is always a great jumble of pots (See page 148.) This shrub rose, 'Gertrude Jekyll', has lived in the same pot for three years, and here shows its second flowering of the season. By bringing the pot into the kitchen in late winter, I have a mass of sweet-scented blooms in early spring, to the delight of all who see it. The nicotianas grow in a bed surrounded by terracotta edging tiles. Sitting on the rug is Maia, one of my four children, holding our brindled lurcher.

Pelargonium tricolor merits a pot on its own. (See page 148.)

In Nepal flowerpots come in many shapes; even lions, toads and elephants. Inspiration for the other pots in this group comes from nearer at hand, with Devon "pastry" work decorating three different styles of pot. (See page 148.)

I exhibited this very large Ali Baba at the Chelsea Flower Show in 1989. In its neck I plunged a small pot full of "mind your own business". It looked so like an unkempt head of hair that by the end of the Show it was flattened by the many pats it had received! The jar is made from three pieces thrown separately and joined together when slightly stiffened. The decoration is inspired by the art of the Sassanian Empire which flourished in Persia and rivalled Constantine's Eastern Empire. (See page 148.)

The weathered surface of this old trendle is mirrored by the soft, feathery texture of Cosmos 'Sensation' given to Andrew by a friend. (See page 149.)

GOTHIC HOUSE
Trendles, crocks and chimney pots

Andrew Lawson

Andrew Lawson took most of the photographs for this book. When I saw his own plantings this summer, I could not resist asking him to be one of the gardeners as well as the photographer. In both fields he uses his artist's training to great effect, and I felt it would be interesting to find out more about his dual approach.

So, one gentle autumn day, we sat on a bench in his garden in Oxfordshire, and I addressed a few questions to him. We started with the old earthenware pots of which Andrew and his wife Briony are so fond, made by the Country Potters of the West Country. "We are very keen on the domestic ware that we find down in Devon where Briony comes from. They were all used in the old farmhouses until recently. We have bread crocks, jugs, bowls and, best of all, what we call 'trendles', which were used for salting pork in brine over the winter. I've got three of them and they are my greatest treasures." With holes bored carefully in the bottom, they become beautiful containers for summer plantings, but because they are well over a century old and beginning to crumble, they are brought indoors every winter.

The Lawsons also like old chimney pots. Briony, who is a sculptress, uses them as bases for her statues, and Andrew likes their shape and height in a grouping of pots. The common or garden flowerpot is there, too, clustered with more unusual neighbours, or plunged into the beds for protecting and growing bulbs.

When it comes to planting, Andrew likes to mass pots near the house. "I do not have terrific regimes of planning for these pots, they just happen. Because of my work as a photographer of gardens I get a lot of cast-offs or presents from peoples' gardens. This", he said, indicating the yellow flowers and trailing branches of a vigorous *Bidens ferulifolia*, "was being thrown out at Hidcote. I was rather pleased to have a plant from Hidcote, reject or not, and it has done terribly well."

Andrew trained as an artist, and his painter's eye does not allow the random approach that his words might imply: "Coming from painting, I have learnt about colour theory, and about the differences between harmonious colour and contrasting colour. I can now see how some gardeners manage to work these colour associations extremely well and others don't. Some people do it instinctively, while others follow a theory, which is what I do. I have some corners of my garden in which I use very closely allied colours, and in other places I make contrasts by putting the opposite colours on the 'colour circle' together – blues with yellows or reds with greens are the strongest, most obvious combinations."

I asked Andrew how he made the transition from being a painter to a garden photographer: "For years I have been a very keen gardener, and until five years ago my main activity in life was as a painter, although I was employed by publishers in various roles, but it was only in 1985 that someone asked me to photograph my first garden. Suddenly – almost like a flash of light – I realized that what I was really interested in I could also do as a job. Since then I have earned my living photographing gardens, which I think must be one of the most pleasurable occupations you can imagine.

"As a garden photographer my whole attitude to gardening changes about every ten minutes because I see everyone else's ideas, and they inspire me to do totally different things with my own garden. There is hardly a plant here which has not been moved at least once, if not twice, to establish some new association.

"I would say that my training and interest in painting has dominated my eye as a photographer, and inevitably it influences the pictures I take of other people's gardens. It is very personal and people are often surprised at the choice of subject. I suppose I am imposing my own eye on somebody else's creation, which is perhaps bad. I think I have fairly catholic tastes, but I have to admit that my photography is very subjective, and if I do not like a thing I probably will not take a picture of it. Unlike me, a good photographer should possibly be completely impersonal and objective.

"Gardening photography has not led, so far, to anything in my painting, but I am definitely hoping some day to find time to bring my love of gardens into that area of my life as well."

Storage jars mingle with old flowerpots and glazed bottles. They are set around two large oval trendles which hold mixed summer plantings. Before using these for plants, Andrew Lawson carefully bored several small drainage holes in the bottom with a hand-drill, best done with the pot upside down on the lawn.

Andrew Lawson's garden is full of incident and colour. On the terrace beside the house, he likes to mass white and fragrant flowers. Their rich green foliage sets off his collection of old terracotta and the grey and golds of the Cotswold walls. (See page 149.) This is the same group of pots shown on the previous page, but taken a month later. The nicotiana have taken over from the lilies which have been deadheaded.

For all their apparent simplicity, trendles are difficult to make; a deep, oval shape was needed to hold a pork leg in brine. This shape can be hand-coiled, but the more usual method is as follows. The side walls and rim are thrown as usual on the wheel, but without a base, and allowed to stiffen slightly. A flat slab of clay is rolled out for the base, and the thrown wall is then transferred onto this, being pushed into the distinctive oval shape before it is fixed down with a coil of damp clay. The handles are added last.

Parsley, chives and mint in a pot just 7 inches high. A few sprigs have been removed for the photographer's lunch.

To make this pot, holes are cut in the side of a freshly-thrown pot, the lower edges of which are then gently eased between the first and second fingers of the hand, giving a lip which later holds back the soil. Care needs to be taken to avoid over-vigorous watering which may cause the soil to be washed out of the holes. This is a small version of a strawberry pot which, standing up to 2 feet high, can look extremely effective with a mixture of alpine plants, as well as with herbs and strawberries. (See page 149.)

A painted pot, using the blue that John created for the benches and gateways of Chilcombe.

CHILCOMBE HOUSE
Painter's paradise

John Hubbard

The hamlet of Chilcombe in Dorset is a magical place. You approach it through a sheltering spinney to find the tiny church and medieval manor house nestling in a south-facing hollow of the hills. Spread out in front of you is a magnificent view over the last of the downs to the sea beyond.

Caryl and John Hubbard came here in 1969. They were initially attracted by the beauty of the house and its setting; creating an exceptional garden was not a conscious part of their plans. "We liked it because it's such an incredible place. We did not give the garden any thought at all. The whole place was collapsing and there were so many other things to deal with that doing the garden was the least of our worries." But they did plant trees early on, so they are now sheltered from the north and the west winds, and the south-easterlies are considerably reduced. Tender plants flourish in sheltered spots by the house, or within the protective walls and leafy alleys of the main garden which follows the divided rectangular layout of the seventeenth-century original.

The Hubbards manage the garden with only a three-day-a-week gardener to help, in spite of being professionally occupied elsewhere. Caryl is a trustee of the National Gallery and actively involved in the Contemporary Art Society, and John is a painter. His near-abstract paintings and drawings speak of a fascination with plants and gardens – the forms and colours of foliage and flowers in a never-ending play of light and shade. Visits to other gardens – he mentions the subtropical gardens of Tresco Abbey, Isles of Scilly, and the Moorish gardens of Spain – provide material for his work and ideas for Chilcombe: "It makes you realize just how limited your own imagination is when you see how other people make things."

In their own garden, the artist's eye is, of course, everywhere apparent. When I admired the planting of scarlet *Salvia elegans* near the deep orange flowers of runner beans, John's enthusiasm for colour took him off on a dissertation on orange: "Don't be afraid of orange. We have Welsh poppies here – the yellow ones and the bright orange ones – and that clear orange will go with just about everything. What does not work are the muddier colours – certain insipid oranges or that colour they call 'flame'."

John gets great pleasure from the surprises of gardening: "Odd things happen just by fluke. Somebody says, 'That's a clever idea', when it was not an idea at all, it just happened. You suddenly see a combination, a relation of things: this is what makes it so exciting."

You would be mistaken to think, however, that the subtle beauties of Chilcombe have been arrived at by chance. I noted that John Hubbard places and uses pots with as much care as he composes the other elements of the garden. In one area a single pot brimming with yellow was placed at the centre of converging paths: the colour was a perfect foil for the bright blue felicia nearby and the size, smaller than one would expect for a focal point, was absolutely matched to the scale of the surrounding beds. Elsewhere he had plunged pots of smaller plants into a permanent planting to add detail and variety.

As John Hubbard talked, deadheading as we walked, about past seasons and plans for the future, I realized how important the creative part of gardening is to him. We started discussing the use of coloured ornament in gardens, like the glorious tiles and glazes of the Arab tradition, and the possibility of painting terracotta as, indeed, our Jacobean and Victorian forebears did. I could see his imagination getting to work – and I knew that the next time I came to Chilcombe there would be fresh delights in store.

After the jasmine had finished flowering, John Hubbard wanted to brighten up this south-facing wall in the courtyard that fronts the oldest part of Chilcombe House. The planting is designed to last the summer through, with the Felicia amelloides having a second flowering in the early autumn.

A plain, well-balanced pot has been chosen as a foil to the complexity of foliage behind and the striking irregularities of the paving below. (See page 150.)

Some gardens are made up of clearly separate elements, relying for effect on the contrast that gives. At Chilcombe the opposite is true.

All the elements are mixed together harmonized by an unerring colour sense. Here espalier fruit trees are festooned with clematis, forming a backdrop to a small parterre full of plants which thrive in a sheltered garden. The pot sits at the crossing of the paths; the still centre in a whirl of colour. (See page 150.)

Imagine the smell of these regal lilies coming through the open windows. Then add the sweet pungency of fennel. In places like this, where one would not want to risk having a damp flowerbed next to the house wall, a line of pots can be a useful way of filling the gap.

Lilies grow particularly well in deep containers but should not be left outside over winter. (See page 150.)

John Hubbard was looking for a specific effect when he immersed this pot in the border. The previous season, he had tried using lilies in smaller pots, but found they were not making the point he wanted. This time, with a larger pot raising the delicate blooms of verbenas and *Sphaeralcea miniata* to prominence, he achieved the results for which he had hoped. (See page 150.)

At the entrance to the splendid Victorian Orangery at Castle Ashby, a large papyrus stands with its feet in the central pool. The pool wall is made from terracotta medallions by Minton. (See page 150.)

CASTLE ASHBY
Victorian grandeur

Joanne Miles

I t was the lamp standards outside Hatfield House – immaculate terra-cotta reproductions after Roman ones found at Hadrian's Villa – which led me to the Victorian terraces of Castle Ashby, Northamptonshire, and to J.M. Blashfield, terracotta manufacturer extraordinaire.

These Victorian extravagances are not to my taste, but no book on terracotta would be complete without mentioning them. Blashfield worked within the "Coade stone" tradition (see page 24) and in his Stamford works he produced a yellowish "terracotta" of exceptional hardness. He was part of the heavy terracotta industry which developed to supply the Victorians' insatiable demand for modelled building ornament. His work at Castle Ashby shows the attention to detail and insistence on top-quality modelling that eventually priced his terracotta out of existence in the face of less scrupulous competition.

In the 1860s he was commissioned by the Marquess of Northampton to manufacture the ornate brickwork and urns for a series of Italian terraces at Castle Ashby. The overall designs were the work of the Marquess and Sir Matthew Digby Wyatt, while detail and practicalities were left to Blashfield. The terraces stretch on various levels from the Jacobean east front of the house towards the lakes and woods of Capability Brown's landscape. They are huge, edged round their outer limits with terracotta balustrading containing biblical quotations in vast capital letters in emula-tion of the stone lettering that runs round the house, and punctuated by highly ornamented pillars. Urns of many designs and sizes, now planted with vivid red and white pelargoniums, dot the lengths of balustrading, and the extravaganza is completed by terracotta fountains. The quality of the workmanship is undoubtedly superb and I enjoyed working out how Blashfield's sculptors had achieved the detailing on the faces, figures, swags and shells, combining moulding with model-ling. But I found myself feeling rather depressed by the endless self-importance and dead perfection of the terraces.

Wyatt also involved Blashfield in the Italian gardens he created on the site of the old kitchen garden, and these are more to my taste. Approaching them from the south, you look down a vista of tall box hedges through Wyatt's triumphal arch to the Orangery, built in 1871–73. The effect evokes some Tuscan villa, and the Orangery is the most beautiful I have ever seen. Joanne Miles, now head gardener, amazed me when she said that its planting dated back only to 1986. "We took all the soil out and changed it for an acid soil because we are alkaline here. We close it all up round about December, and don't go in there until February to try and keep the frost out."

The last seven years at Castle Ashby have seen the beginnings of a gradual restoration of the gardens, and this year staff were increased to a total of four. Borders are now being planted again, but

much of the colour is provided by the one hundred and sixty seven terracotta urns that are refilled every year. Rows of deep Doulton urns lead up to the Orangery – Blashfield had been forced out of business by the time they were needed. As Joanne explains: "The spiky foliage of a *Cordyline* surrounded by the intense red blooms of petunias provides a theme to connect the pots. Last year we used trailing pink geraniums, but I prefer the stronger contrast of the red against the greens of the grass and the trees."

Blashfield's terracottas put me in mind of Vasari, talking about over-decoration and high finish in his *Life* of Luca della Robbia: "The vulgar prefer a certain external and apparent delicacy, where the lack of what is essential is concealed by the care bestowed, to a good work produced with reason and judgement but not so smooth or so highly finished."

Another generation will no doubt disagree, and I hope the present efforts at restoring the grand terraces manage to preserve them for the future.

Each leaf and fruit of the swags on this Blashfield urn has been individually applied with his usual meticulous attention to detail. Like Coade stone, whose formula Blashfield adapted to produce his own distinctive pale yellow terracotta, the forms have lost none of their crispness in the last hundred years.

The interior of the Orangery, built in 1871-73 to Sir Matthew Digby Wyatt's design. Unusually, it has windows to the north side, allowing one to see right through to the Capability Brown landscape beyond .

An excellent example of an old English pot of red terracotta. It is a handcoiled pot and closely follows Italian models. The decoration has been beautifully executed using a number of small moulds, and applied after making. This magnificent begonia is cut back each winter and transferred to a heated greenhouse. (See page 151.)

A riotous mixture of reds and pinks overruns a baroque urn. The original was made to go in the restored seventeenth-century gardens at Ham House in Twickenham, Middlesex. (See page 151.)

SOUTHVIEW
Tuscan splendour

Rupert Golby

I have to admit my bias; Rupert Golby helped me with the plantings for my new courtyard garden this year as well as with some big pots for Chelsea, and I think he does a wonderful job. Trained at the Royal Horticultural Society's Garden at Wisley and the Royal Botanic Gardens, Kew, he worked for some time in Italy at Ninfa, a luxuriant "English" garden fed by mountain springs and set in the ruins of an eighth-century town, cataloguing their collection of plants. On his return, he spent several years creating his first professional garden at a house near Oxford, and then worked with Rosemary Verey at Barnsley House. He now runs his own landscape design business.

Rupert is still disconcertingly young. He has acquired a great knowledge of plants, and his distinctive style of planting unites a relaxed euphoria with tasteful restraint. He likes the contrast between formality and informality: "In a garden as a whole I like to combine a formal layout – box hedges, straight paths and clipped edges – with an informal planting. It works the same way with a classical pot, if you then use a full, overflowing style."

Rupert first came across decorative terracotta at one of the Royal Horticultural Society's Shows in Vincent Square, London. It was being displayed by Anne Reddington, who used to import traditional hand-made pots from Tuscany. From then on, he became a regular customer in her two shops, sadly now both gone.

Terracotta is very popular with his clients, especially once they see how well it can mellow. He finds that when the pots have developed a patina with age they stand equally well against stonework or brick.

In his container plantings Rupert displays a penchant for small-flowered half-hardy annuals and tender perennials mixed in harmonious colours with a good helping of interesting foliage. "I do like subtle plantings. I think it takes years and years of practice to succeed with strong reds, yellows and blues. It is much easier to start off using muted pinks, pale blues and white with lots of silver foliage. Once you have more experience, then you can start to add brighter colours. It is experimentation really – you find good ideas in other people's gardens and then see how you can work them through in your own plantings."

Working as he does in a variety of gardens, Rupert has to be responsive to the special demands and qualities of each location. He emphasizes the importance of being "appropriate to the site" when placing a pot. "You have to look and see where you can put containers to have the most impact. In its own way, a big urn is a major planting, like a flowering shrub or a tree, and it can be used as a focal point. And I do not mean simply at the end of an avenue; pots can be set against shrubs, or in the corner of a garden. They can quite easily be fitted in with a permanent feature, like when you train ivies or a wisteria against a wall leaving some of the surface exposed you can put a wall pot in that gap. With the unexpected contrast, it can be an amusing surprise."

As well as giving thought to the site, Rupert has to take into account the diverse requirements of his clients. "Pots are ideal for busy or elderly gardeners who may have big gardens without much flower because they cannot manage a herbaceous border. By using flowerpots on a stone terrace, or around the back door, you can get some wonderful effects close to the house, and they only take a moment to look after.

"With a pot one can create a small garden which is flowering constantly throughout the summer. I know people who have three or four duplicate pots. They keep some in reserve so that when the first ones are over, they simply bring out the others to replace them in the same spot. It may be that they only have room for one tub or one urn, but they will swop them to get a good display from early spring to the end of autumn."

These pots are so magnificent that the sparseness of the new box hedging is hardly noticed. The pale Italian terracotta goes well with the blue-greens of an old copper in the centre. Rupert Golby prefers pale tones, and he uses them here with with vivid pink verbena to connect the plantings together. Pots can create an eye-catching show in a new garden while more permanent features get under way.(See page 151.)

The fluted curves of this urn are plunged into the enveloping branches of a viburnum. For all its romantic arcadianism, this use of a striking pot has many practical points to recommend it. Once the viburnum has finished flowering, colour and interest are provided by summer bedding plants. In winter, the urn stands revealed in all its detail. In its leafy niche, it is unlikely to get blown over.

This pot came from Italy seven years ago, and is made in two pieces, so that the top lifts off the pedestal. This design is more commonly found in stone, and the classical originals were made either of marble or beaten metal. (See page 152.)

This finely-modelled trough from Impruneta in Italy is adapted from the pagan sarcophagi of the Romans and Etruscans. Garlands and cherubs are echoed by the ebullience of a planting, in which only the colour is controlled. A light frothy effect comes from only using plants with small leaves and flowers. It is a surprise to see how well this ornate piece looks in a simple setting – neither an orangery nor a grand vista are necessary to indulge in spectacular terracotta. (See page 152.)

The loud, Victorian chequer-board brickwork has here been forced into the background by choosing plants with even brighter tonal contrasts: pillar-box red geraniums with dark green foliage. The effect almost glows in the dark. (See page 152.)

A simple spring planting of blue pansies and white tulips suits the elegance of these beautiful handpressed pots. They are made from Renaissance designs in Impruneta, Italy. Later in the season, they will be cleared to make way for a summer display. (See page 153.)

*A homeless variegated aralia was the starting point for what Rupert Golby calls
"a study in green and white". (See page 153.)*

*A yellow argyranthemum and Bidens aurea peep out from a golden-leaved hop (Humulus lupulus Aureus')
growing against a stone wall. Wallpots look good tucked among climbers, where they add colour and variety.
(See page 153).*

CHAPTER THREE

THE TERRACOTTA PLANTINGS

I n the first chapter of this book I talked of the history and making of terracotta. Then I showed pots used in many different ways and as many styles of planting. Now I shall briefly describe how to choose a pot, plant it and keep it looking well.

For many years, my own flowerpots have held only single species, not in the least complicated to deal with. So I approached the more complex plantings in this book with a sense of awe and the feeling that they were way beyond my understanding.

After much patient explaining on the part of my contributors, I am, however, now ready to pass on their knowledge to anyone who feels similarly daunted. In fact, the creation of subtle plantings is a microcosm of larger-scale gardening, and as soon as a few basic rules have been grasped, you are away into the realm of personal expression, limited only by your knowledge of flowering plants. The success of the enterprise is, as always in gardening, a reflection of how well and how regularly the plants are then tended.

After a discussion of the technicalities of terracotta and its uses, there follow here the details of each planting illustrated in Chapter Two. As well as the names and numbers of plants used, a description of each gardener's favoured potting compost is given. Each pot is detailed together with its source and age if known, and this information can be used in conjunction with the List of Suppliers on page 156.

The characteristics of terracotta

Garden terracotta is fired at the relatively low temperature of 1,000°C (1,832°F) and is a type of "earthenware". At this temperature, it has not begun to melt together, like a crude glass, as it would if you fired it higher, and so it remains fairly porous.

Plants grow well in terracotta pots. Roots need air as well as moisture, and can breathe through the porous walls of a clay pot. The evaporation of water from the outside of the pot in hot weather keeps the rootball inside relatively cool. And in winter the terracotta gives more insulation than many other materials.

The fact that the clay remains porous, and so contains water, makes it susceptible to frost. Amazingly, damage need not occur if good raw materials are used, prepared properly, and then fired to a sufficiently high temperature. Good manufacturers offer a guarantee against lamination in the frost, even if the pot is left planted up all winter. You need beware only if the shape of the pot encloses the earth, as in an "ali baba" jar. With an ordinary flared shape, the compost can slide upwards as it expands during freezing, whereas in an enclosed shape it may stay trapped, and split the pot in two. If in doubt, the pot should be half-emptied of compost in the last days of autumn and not used for permanent plantings.

Machine-made pots often fall apart in the frost. The most common cause is that the clay has been inadequately prepared before being formed into a pot. When pots are made by hand, clay has to be prepared well or it is impossible to use; a machine is not so choosy.

Fired terracotta is usually orange, though it may also be red or yellow. Wood firing and, to a lesser extent, gas and oil bring out subtle variations in the basic colour. Like all good materials, it grows more beautiful with age, acquiring a patina built up with salts from the clay and potting compost, algae and general dirt.

It takes only a few weeks or months for most terracotta to mellow, but for those who cannot wait there are several ways to speed up the natural weathering process. The colour of a pot can be lightened with a wash of lime. It can be made greener by a regular spray with liquid fertilizer, or brushing with water in which has been soaked either manure or comfrey leaves. Some people use yoghurt or old milk, and I find dripping trees, or gutters, and long grass, soon mellow the brightest colour. The main thing in "ageing" a pot is to keep it damp, and not to be impatient: a good pot will last for many years.

The positioning of pots

I hope the illustrations in this book show how versatile flowerpots can be. Pots can be magnificent in formal surroundings, pointing up patterns, astride a wall or flanking a flight of steps. But I am particularly excited by more informal uses, where pots are grouped together to create a new focus or area of interest, perhaps transforming a boring eyesore into something special.

Pots are, after all, moveable and this is one of their greatest assets and the source of much fun. If you have a selection of planted pots it is quick work to conjure up a fresh effect in a new place. So do not be too stuck in your ways about where they should live.

Pots can also be used to help overcome extreme climates and broaden the range of plants that can be grown. Every garden has hot and cold corners, and shady or sunny areas, and pots may be planted to make special use of these microclimates.

Choosing a pot

The position that a pot is to occupy must affect the choice of shape and style, particularly if the setting is formal. Size will be important, as it is when matching a pot to an existing specimen planting.

Mostly, though, choice of shape is a matter of personal taste. Some people prefer clean, simple lines and often go for plain horticultural ware, while others enjoy the ebullient cornucopias swathing the sides of a Renaissance urn. Personally, I love both extremes, and find that they enhance each other, the plain offering a cool foil to the more ornate.

Pots look particularly well *en masse*, with or without plants, their different shapes and sizes complementing each other. If in doubt, it is always worth buying as large a pot as possible, for this holds the most possibilities for an exciting planting.

I have hardly mentioned machine-made terracotta pots in this book, because I do not like them. They cost less than hand-made pots, although considering their poorer quality, not a lot less. I urge close inspection before buying any, as I have yet to see a really good machine-produced design. In addition, there is always the fear that they will fall apart in frosty weather, and machine-made pots are often so smooth that they will never acquire the beautiful patina of good terracotta.

132

In an out-of-the-way corner of the gardens of Castle Ashby stands this Blashfield urn, surrounded by a grove of uncut yew trees. (See page 151).

How do you tell a hand-made pot? A pot made on the wheel will always have throwing rings spiralling up the inside of the pot. A hand-pressed pot will be fairly heavy, and show many small imperfections outside and tool or finger marks inside. A hand-built pot will always be quite irregular and uneven.

Being hand-made is, alas, no guarantee of a pot being beautiful! Even the best potters have bad days, and in the end you have to choose the pots you like.

Potting composts

Shirley Hibberd, a prolific and popular Victorian author and gardening journalist, wrote charmingly about potting composts: "Composts for plant-growing are compounded in a great many different ways, as patent medicines are; but the wise cultivator will not have many of them. We will suppose that the bins (in your potting shed) are filled with materials. These should consist of mellow loam full of decayed fibre, tough fibrous peat, silver sand, leaf mould, potsherds, old broken plaster or mortar, and the most rotten portion of the manure from an old hotbed or any similar source. With these before us, we will prepare what will henceforth be termed the 'universal compost', and upon my word, if you never deviate from this prescription, you may become an expert plant-grower and a winner of first prizes."

I will make no such assumptions about the state of your "bins", and instead suggest that you attain your first prizes by simpler means.

The first choice to be made is between a soil- or loam-based potting compost, and a soil-less one, usually made out of peat. General-purpose peat-based composts are popular because they are light, clean to use, and water-retentive if not allowed to dry out completely. However, if you travel to the bogs of Ireland, Somerset or East Anglia, you cannot fail to notice the serious damage being done by commercial peat extraction. So, I try to use a compost with as little peat as possible in its formulation.

I use the various loam-based John Innes mixtures. This is not a brand name but the name of the

Horticultural Research Institution in Merton, England, where a basic compost was created which, if slightly modified, would suit most plants grown in pots. This mix consists of seven parts sterilized loam (stacked for at least one year); three parts peat; and two parts coarse lime-free sand. To this is added a standard fertilizer mixture, traditionally consisting of two parts hoof and horn (for nitrogen); two parts superphosphate of lime, and one part sulphate of potash.

By increasing the amount of fertilizer mixture, the strength of the basic compost can be varied: No. 1 contains 4 oz of fertilizer per bushel of compost and is recommended for seedlings and slow growers; No. 2 contains 8 oz per bushel and is multi-purpose, suitable for most plants; and No. 3 has 12 oz per bushel, a strong mixture for vigorous growers and climbers. In addition, a small amount of ground chalk or limestone is added to each compost making them unsuitable for lime-hating plants such as rhododendrons and camellias. For these a modified ericaceous (lime-free) compost should be used.

Plants that need good drainage, such as alpines, cacti, and other succulents, will benefit from a generous helping of extra grit, or coarse sand, mixed into ordinary potting compost.

Many of the gardeners featured in this book make their own potting mix, following similar proportions to the John Innes formula. Some buy their ingredients – sterilized loam, peat and washed coarse sand; others use their own ingredients. Mrs Franks remembered the days before she could get hold of peat. She would stagger back from the woods with sacks of well-rotted bracken, and use the tilth of molehills for loam. Leaf mould is another excellent alternative.

Organic potting composts are available. If you have difficulty getting some locally, they are available by mail order.

Vermiculite or perlite can be added to a compost to help water-retention. At Tintinhull they use a water-retaining gel, which is soaked before being added, and this may soon be available to the amateur gardener.

Most potting composts already contain the nutrients that your plants will need to get off to a good start, but there is no harm in adding slow-release fertilizer in the form of granules, pellets or sticks. Bonemeal, which is slow to dissolve in water, is also a good option. At Hatfield, where they garden organically, they put a layer of well-rotted farmyard manure at the bottom of the pot.

Rupert Golby uses pots to emphasize scale. This huge urn with its satyrs' heads, acanthus leaves and overflowing cornucopia matches the elegant grandeur of a Georgian country house. Formality is softened by plantings of unruly greenery. (See page 153).

Potting technique

All plants need good drainage. If their rootball gets waterlogged for any length of time, most plants will rot and die. So all flowerpots have holes in the base or lower side. Before any compost is put in them, the bottom of the pot should be covered with a layer of broken pot, stones or coarse gravel. In large pots, a layer of gravel on top of the broken crocks further improves drainage, although the gravel used should not be too fine or it can be washed through and clog up the hole in the bottom of the pot.

When potting up plants, shrubs or trees which are going to be kept in pots for years, be sure not to over-pot. As a plant grows, it will need repotting during its early years, but a large shrub can be grown in a surprisingly small container. Every autumn after its second year the plant should be removed from its pot, and either "potted on" into a larger pot giving a couple of inches or so more room all round, or root pruned. When it is dry, you can be quite violent to the rootball of a dormant plant, removing a lot of old, used-up compost, and pulling away some of the chunks of matted roots. The gardeners at Versailles used to attack their dormant orange trees with scythe blades, cutting away slithers of compacted root all round the exposed ball. Root pruning finished, the plant would be packed back into its old pot with fresh drainage crocks and new compost worked in around its roots.

Putting a flowering or fruiting shrub in too large a pot stimulates excess root growth. By mid-summer the roots of the plant should fill the pot, forcing its energies into producing flowers or fruit rather than ever more roots.

Tender bedding plantings are quite different. Here the secret is to pack in as many plants as possible – witness the planting lists of Mrs Merton on page 136. Much plant material can be bought from nurseries and garden centres in late spring for planting out. This can be used as a source of cuttings for next year or just left to be killed by the autumn frost before clearing away.

With a greenhouse it is possible to keep one's own stock of tender plants going from year to year. This is not as difficult as it might sound. Some bedding plants grow easily from their own seed, collected when ripe and sown in mid-winter in the greenhouse. For plants whose seed does not set or highly bred plants such as fuchsia cultivars, take a few small cuttings in late summer or early autumn and plant them in a mixture of peat and coarse sand in equal parts. The ideal is to make up a small bed of this mixture on a greenhouse bench, with a heating cable immersed in the compost to stimu-late good root growth. You do not want the plants to grow many new leaves until late winter, or they will need potting on too soon, and so the cuttings should be well ventilated with the greenhouse door kept open during any sunny days. The frost must, however, be kept out. The leaves of the cuttings should be kept moist by a regular misting of water in all but the coldest weather. They need very little water to survive, especially if the moisture is trapped round them with a clear plastic "oxygen tent" rigged up to cover the bed. Alterna-tively, use a heated propagating case. The vents should be opened during the day but in such a close environment the amount of watering will be less than on the greenhouse bench.

Pot the rooted cuttings into 3-inch or 4-inch pots in late winter, and by late spring they should be bursting, ready to pot up together outside once all danger of frost has passed.

The pots used for summer bedding displays can already have been working hard, showing off spring bulbs planted the autumn before. It pays to experiment with mixing early and late flowering species or cultivars, or to plant bulbs of the same kind at three different depths in the compost to prolong flowering time.

Aftercare – watering, feeding and deadheading

There are exceptions, but most plants do not like their roots either to dry out or to be waterlogged, preferring them to be just damp. To achieve this in a flowerpot, the weather must be taken into account. In the cool of spring and autumn, a weekly watering may be enough, but in high summer heat, daily soakings will be needed.

As a general rule, if you are watering, do it properly. Fill up the space at the top of the pot until you can see water running out of the bottom. In hot weather, evening or early morning is the best time for watering, as the extremes of midday wettings send plants into shock.

All that water flowing through the compost soon leaches out its goodness, so regular feeding is essential to keep plants in good condition. Some people use a handful of slow-release fertilizer sprinkled on the surface of the compost, but I prefer a weekly liquid feed, which nourishes through the leaves as well as the roots. Feeding should only be carried out during the growing season, and stopped in late summer, especially for perennials. Otherwise they may put on extra new growth which will not have time to harden off before the winter.

Many tender perennials and bedding plants will flower all summer long if deadheaded regularly. This simple operation prevents the formation of seeds and thus encourages more flowers as well as keeping the display tidy. However, towards the end of the season seedheads can be allowed to develop if seeds are required for the following year. These should be collected in brown paper bags, labelled and kept in a tin somewhere cool and dry until the following spring.

Key to the plantings

If I had to point to one characteristic shared by all my contributors, I would choose inventiveness. These details of the plantings shown in Chapter Two are one season's ideas, and if you looked at the same pots next year, some would be the same, but many would show new ideas and fresh plants. Gardeners are great borrowers, always on the look-out for unusual flowers or different combinations to take home and adapt to their own ends. This section is to be used just like that, as a source of inspiration.

Pots are illustrated wherever foliage obscures their shape in the photograph. Although not drawn to scale, the dimensions of each pot are always given. The number in brackets indicates the style of a Whichford pot. The numbers and names of plants used in a display follow the key numbers in the left-hand margin.

THE OLD RECTORY   *Pages 36, 38–45*
Mrs Merton

For all her magnificent summer displays Mrs Merton uses the same potting mixture. To a weak loam-based potting compost (John Innes No. 1) she adds Irish moss peat and perlite to trap more moisture.

Between July and mid-September she applies a liquid feed once a week to all her pots.

Photograph on page 36

POT   Height 27 inches, width 10 inches

Origin   probably an Italian pot for olive oil.
Age   50 years plus

PLANTING   *Photographed 21 July*
A summer display of tender perennials planted out in late spring.
Position   sunny

Plants
3 *Verbena* 'Sissinghurst'
2 ivy-leaf *Pelargonium* Harlequin series

Photograph on page 38

POT   Height 19½ inches, width 27 inches

Origin   Whichford (622B)
Age   new

PLANTING   *Photographed 21 July*
A summer display of half-hardy plants and bulbs planted out in late spring.
Position   sunny

Key to plants
1.   1 *Agave americana* 'Variegata'
2.   3 *Lilium* Citronella Strain
3.   3 *Helichrysum petiolare* 'Limelight'
4.   3 *Bidens aurea*
5.   5 *Verbena* 'Loveliness'
6.   2 *Argyranthemum frutescens* 'Jamaica Primrose'
7.   1 *Tibouchina semidecandra*
8.   2 *Euphorbia mellifera*
9.   1 *Hosta plantaginea*
10.   1 *Abutilon* 'Canary Bird'
11.   teazels *(Dipsacus sylvestris)* planted in border

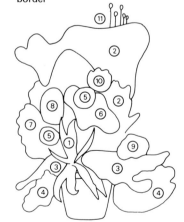

Photograph on pages 40–41

POT – left Height 19½ inches, width 27 inches

Origin   Whichford (621B)
Age   one year

PLANTING   *Photographed 21 July*
A summer display of half-hardy annuals and tender perennials planted out in late spring.
Position   sunny

Key to plants
1.   1 *Fuchsia boliviana*
2.   1 *Cordyline australis*
3.   5 *Verbena* 'Loveliness' (pale form)
4.   5 red, single ivy-leaf trailing pelargoniums
5.   3 *Helichrysum petiolare* 'Variegatum'
6.   3 *Verbena peruviana*
7.   3 red petunias
8.   2 *Pelargonium* x *kewensis*

Photograph on page 42

POT   Height 20 inches, width 20 inches

Origin   bought in a sale many years ago. Traditional English.
Age   40 years plus

PLANTING   *Photographed 21 July*
A summer display of tender perennials planted out in late spring.
Position   sunny

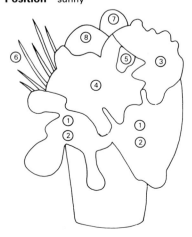

Key to plants

1. 5 pink semi-double ivy-leaf pelargoniums
2. 3 *Helichrysum microphyllum*
3. 1 *Argyranthemum foeniculaceum* pink form
4. 1 *Senecio maritima* 'Cirrus'
5. 5 *Verbena* 'Du Barri'
6. 1 *Phormium* 'Purpureum'
7. 1 *Fuchsia* 'Lottie Hobby'

Photograph on page 43 – top

POT A	**POT B**
Height 9 inches	8½ inches
Width 12½ inches	14 inches

Origin

Whichford (902)	Whichford (half orange)

Age

new	new

PLANTING *Photographed 21 July*

A summer display of hardy and half-hardy foliage plants. These were planted out in late spring when all fear of frost was gone.

Position shade

Key to plants

1. 1 *Helichrysum petiolare* 'Limelight'
2. 2 *Tolmiea menziesii* 'Taff's Gold'
3. 1 *Matteuccia struthiopteris*
4. *Hosta* cv.
5. *Bamusa* dwarf species
6. *Nicotiana suaveolens* 'Hopley's'

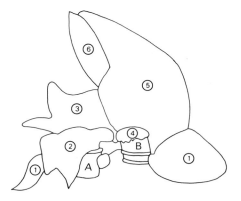

Photograph on page 44

POT A	**POT B**
Height 8 inches	13 inches
Width 17 inches	14 inches

Origin

Whichford (2022)	Whichford (502B)

Age

new	new

PLANTING *Photographed 21 July*

A display of tender perennials and half-hardy annuals planted out in late spring.

Position sunny

Key to plants

Pot A

1. 2 *Brachycome iberidifolia*
2. 3 *Pelargonium* 'Millfield Gem'
3. 4 *Pelargonium* 'L'Elegante'
4. 4 *Heliotropium* Marine

Pot B

1. 1 *Cordyline* 'Purpureum'
2. 3 *Fuchsia* 'Tom West'
3. 3 dark blue petunias
4. 3 pale yellow arctotis

Photograph on page 45

POT	Height 19½ inches, width 27 inches

Origin Whichford (621B)

Age 1 year

PLANTING *Photographed 21 July*

A summer display of tender perennials planted out in late spring.

Position sunny

Key to plants

1. 1 *Cordyline australis*
2. 2 *Salvia fulgens*
3. 2 *Verbena*
4. 5 red, single ivy-leaf pelargoniums
5. 2 *Fuchsia* 'Chang'
6. 3 *Helichrysum petiolare* 'Variegatum'
7. 1 *Lavandula dentata*

POWIS CASTLE
Pages 46–55

Jimmy Hancock

At Powis Castle a loam-based compost is made up to the original John Innes formula (see page 133) with the addition of a slow-release balanced fertilizer. Such a mixture will provide enough nutrients to keep the plants flourishing during the whole of the summer and make liquid feeding in the height of the growing season unnecessary.

Photograph on page 46

POT   Height 20 inches, width 17 inches

Origin   possibly Great Britain. Many of these original Edwardian-Italian terrace pots are still in use but about five years ago replicas were made by Gwen Heany of Ginkgo Clay.

Age   Edwardian

PLANTING   *Photographed 4 July*

A summer display of fuchsias planted up in early April. (Each pot has been planted identically.)

Position   terrace steps leading to the Orangery.

Plants

1 *Fuchsia* 'Mission Bells' (upright)
5 *Fuchsia* 'Eva Boerge' (pendulous)

Photograph on pages 48–49 and 51 – left

POT – see above

Age   modern replica

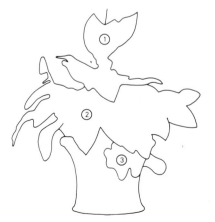

Photograph on page 50

POT – see above

Age   modern replica

PLANTING   *Photographed 4 July*

A summer display of tender perennials and fuchsias planted out early in April.

Position   the Orangery terrace facing south-east

Key to Plants

1. 1 *Fuchsia* 'Tom Woods'
2. 4 *Fuchsia* 'Norman Hutchinson'
3. 3 *Calocephalus brownii*

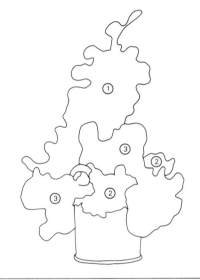

PLANTING   *Photographed 4 July*

A display of perennials planted out in April.

Position   semi-shade at the end of the Yew walk near the entrance to the woodland garden

Key to plants

1. 1 *Canna iridifolia*
2. 5 *Hosta sieboldiana* var. *elegans*
3. 4 lobelia

Photograph on page 51 – right

POT – see above

Age   Edwardian

PLANTING   *Photographed 4 July*

A summer display of tender perennials and half-hardy shrubs planted out early in April.

Position   sheltered terrace facing south-east

Key to plants

1. 1 *Datura (knightii) cornigera*
2. 4 *Argyranthemum frutescens* 'Jamaica Primrose'
3. 3 *Fuchsia fulgens* 'Mary'
4. 6 *Nierembergia repens*

Photographs on pages 52–54

POTS   Height 20 inches, width 18 inches

Origin   Mike O'Brien of Ginkgo Clay, custom-made to fit the niches
Age   3 years

PLANTING   *Photographed 4 July*
A summer display of bedding plants and tender perennials planted up in early April.
Position   below castle on top terrace facing south-east

Key to plants on page 52
1.   1 *Melianthus major*
2.   3 *Fuchsia fulgens* 'Korallie'
3.   3 *Tropaeolum majus* 'Hermine Gnashof'
4.   3 *Helichrysum petiolare*

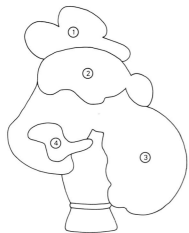

Key to plants on page 53
1.   1 *Salvia guaranitica*
2.   3 *Fuchsia* 'Gartenmeister Bonstedt'
3.   3 *Bidens ferulifolia*
4.   3 *Pelargonium* 'The Boat'

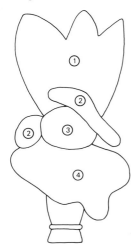

Key to plants on page 54
1.   1 *Lotus berthelotii*
2.   3 trailing lobelia
3.   1 *Corokia x virgata*
4.   3 *Pelargonium* 'The Boat'
5.   2 *Artemesia arborescens*

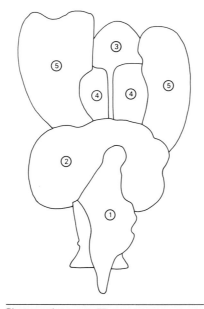

Photograph on page 55

POT   Height 21 inches, width 17½ inches

Origin   Vase Lyonnais made by Emil Henri et fils, Marcigny, France
Age   12 years

PLANTING   *Photographed 4 July*
A summer display of tender perennials and a fuchsia planted out in early April.
Position   sunny

Key to plants
1.   5 *Diascia rigescens*
2.   5 *Helichrysum petiolare*
3.   1 *Fuchsia* 'Joy Patmore'

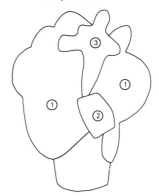

HATFIELD HOUSE   *Pages 56–63*
Lady Salisbury

For David Beaumont, head gardener, arriving at the organically-run garden of Hatfield House was a bit of a shock after his training with a conventional London borough. "There we had a ten-day spraying programme in the central nursery. When I got here, they told me: 'Oh, we don't use any of that.' I thought it would never work, but it does."

He used a strong loam-based compost. When potting up he makes sure that the container is well crocked at the bottom and puts in a generous layer of farmyard manure. For summer feeding they use a 200-gallon drum which goes on the back of a small tractor. It is filled with sea-weed-based liquid feed and used to water all the pots at least once a week and in a dry spell once a day.

Photograph on pages 56 and 58–59

POT   Height 19½ inches, width 27 inches

Origin   Whichford (626B special)
Age   new

PLANTING   *Photographed 27 July*
Permanent planting of perennial herbs, originally planted up in the spring.

Position   sunny

Key to plants
1.   4 *Salvia officinalis* 'Purpurascens'
2.   3 *Origanum majorana*

Photograph on page 60 – top

POTS AND PLANTS *Photographed 27 July*
Each pot is planted with a single tender subject for permanent display.

Summer position sunny, outdoors
Winter position frost-free greenhouse

POT A Height 15 inches, width 21 inches

Origin Whichford (906)
Plant *Citrus* 'Meyer's Lemon'

POT B Height 10 inches, width 12 inches

Origin French
Plant *Plumbago*

POT C Height 11 inches, width 15½ inches

Origin Whichford (904)
Plant Navel orange

POT D Height 8 inches, width 9 inches

Origin traditional English
Plant *Nerium oleander*

POT E Height 10 inches, width 12 inches

Origin French
Plant *Agapanthus*

POT F Height 11 inches, width 15 inches

Origin Whichford (1421)
Plant scented-leaf pelargonium

POT G Height 21½ inches, width 13½ inches

Origin Whichford (602)
Plant *Bidens aurea*

POT H Height 13½ inches, width 18½ inches

Origin Whichford (1422)
Plant *Citrus* 'Meyer's Lemon'

POT I Height 10 inches, width 16 inches

Origin Impruneta
Plant Navel orange

Photograph on page 60 – bottom

POT Height 12 inches, width 15 inches

Origin Hampshire
Age 5 years

PLANTING *Photographed 27 July*
A permanent planting replaced every two to three years in the spring.
Position sunny

Plants 3 or 4 clove carnations per pot

BEECH CROFT ROAD *Pages 64–67*
Mrs Dexter
Mrs Dexter's alpines need especially good drainage, for which she makes up the following compost: two parts coarse sand and two parts leaf mould or peat to one part soil-based potting compost. Pieces of tufa are placed between the plants large enough to touch the bottom of the container. Coarse sand is sprinkled over the surface to ensure the rosettes of foliage do not have to sit in the wet.

Overhead watering is needed all through the summer months using a watering-can with a rose, either in the early morning or the evening.

Photograph on page 66 – top

POT Height 5 inches, width 8 x 17 inches

Origin Oxford
Age 3 years

PLANTING *Photographed 22 June*
Permanent display planted three years ago.
Position sunny

Key to plants
1. *Sempervivum arachnoideum*
2. *Sempervivum braunii*
3. *Sempervivum* 'Purdy'
4. *Sedum spathulifolium* 'Cappa Blanca'
5. *Sedum lydium*
6. *Saxifraga* x *irvingii* 'Jenkinsae'

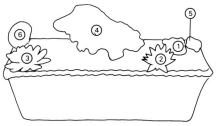

Photograph on page 66 – bottom

POT Height 5 inches, width 13 inches

Origin Middle Barton Pottery
Age 7 years

PLANTING *Photographed 22 June*

Plant *Sempervivum calcareum* 'Sir William Lawrence'

Photograph on page 67 – top

POT   Height 5 inches, six legs, width 17½ inches
Origin   Whichford
Age   2 years

PLANTING   *Photographed 22 June*
A permanent display planted out two years ago.
Position   sunny

Key to plants
1. *Sempervivum arachnoideum*
2. *Sempervivum braunii*
3. *Sempervivum marmoreum (schlehanii)* var. *rubrifolium*
4. *Jovibarva (Sempervivum) soboliferum*
5. *Sedum spathulifolium* 'Purpureum'
6. *Saxifraga paniculata* 'Baldensis'
7. *Saxifraga valdensis*

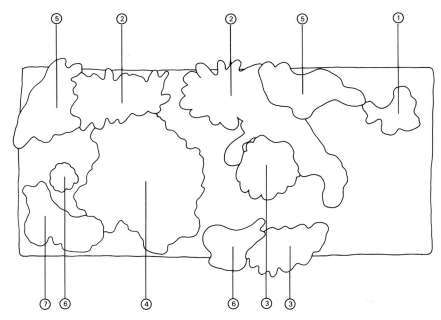

SOUTHSIDE   *Pages 68–73*
Mrs Connie Franks

I asked Mrs Franks what she used for her pots before peat and potting composts became readily available in the shops: "I tell you what I used to do. I would go over to the Dean, the woods here, and I used to take two sacks and get no end of rotted bracken. I didn't even take a wheelbarrow. I would take one bag so far, half way up the street, and then I used to go back and get the other one. You wouldn't be beaten, you know, not if you wanted anything. There used to be summer raspberries . . . I expect there still are.

"But let me tell you the finest thing. Of course I could never find any moles in here, but old Roy Ridge, over the road here, his field used to be full of molehills – now they've got horses and so you don't get moles anymore. But that's the best stuff to plant anything in. Definitely. It's all so lovely and fine. Mix that with a bit of peat or bracken and sand and some feed, and away you go."

These days Mrs Franks uses "mostly peat and a bit of loam – soil stuff. Bonemeal I usually plonk in. Sand sometimes, depends what I'm growing."

Photograph on page 70

POT A	**POT B**
Height 8 inches	12 inches
Width 16 inches	12 inches

Origin
Jonathan Garrett   Mark Griffiths
Age
new   new

PLANTING   *Photographed 26 July*
Summer display planted out in early summer.
Position   sunny
Compost   multi-purpose peat-based compost mixed with Irish moss peat
Fertilizer   liquid tomato fertilizer applied once every three weeks

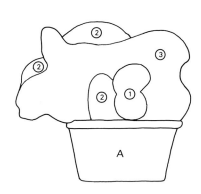

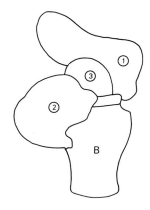

Key to plants
Pot A
1. 1 *Fuchsia* 'Pink Rock'
2. 2 *Senecio maritima*
3. 2 salmon-pink pelargoniums

Pot B
1. 2 *Pelargonium* 'Mrs H. Cox'
2. 8 *Nemesia* mixed colours
3. 2 *Ageratum*, a tall cultivar

Photograph on page 71

POT A   **POT B**

Height 7 inches   7 inches

Width 8 inches   14 inches

Origin

Whichford (335)   Whichford (108)

                  – raised on a Victorian

                  chimney pot

Age

new   new

PLANTING   *Photographed 26 July*

A display of summer bedding, planted at the beginning of summer.

Position   sunny

Compost   multi-purpose peat-based

Fertilizer   liquid tomato feed applied once every three weeks

Key to plants
Pot A

1.   6 pink godetias

Pot B

1.   4 orange pelargoniums
2.   6 tagetes (mixed)
3.   3 variegated mint
4.   3 lobelia
5.   *Cerastium* (around pot)

Photograph on page 72

POT   Height 6 inches, width 10 inches

Origin   Whichford (802)

Age   new

PLANTING   *Photographed 26 July*

A summer display planted out in late spring.

Position   sunny

Compost   multi-purpose peat-based compost with added Irish moss peat

Fertilizer   liquid tomato fertilizer applied once every three weeks

Key to plants

1.   1 *Helichrysum petiolare*
2.   4 *Dimorphotheca chrysanthemifolia*
3.   2 red pelargoniums with variegated foliage

Photograph on page 73

POT   Height 5 inches, width 12 inches square

Origin   Sankeys

Age   at least 70 years

PLANTING   *Photographed 26 July*

A summer display planted up in the first month of summer.

Position   semi-shade

Compost   Irish moss peat

Fertilizer   balanced fertilizer in tablet form

Key to plants

1.   tuberous begonias
2.   1 variegated mint
3.   pelargoniums

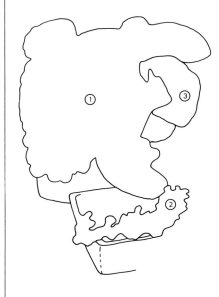

WOODROYD
Pages 74–79

Alan Titchmarsh

Alan Titchmarsh uses a loam-based compost for all his plantings. Permanent displays need the extra nutrients of a strong compost (John Innes No. 3), while his pots of daffodils, tulips and lilies are given one of medium strength (John Innes No. 2) with a little extra sharp sand to aid drainage.

Photograph on page 74

POT   Height 22 inches, width 30 inches

Origin   Whichford (621A)
Age   new

PLANTING   *Photographed 6 September*
A permanent display of topiary.
Position   full sun in a border
Compost   1:1 mixture of loam-based and multi-purpose peat-based composts
Fertilizer   a general purpose liquid feed applied once a fortnight between May and September

Plants
3 *Buxus sempervirens* trimmed to shape

Photograph on page 76

POT   Height 6 inches, width 12 inches

Origin   Whichford (2021)
Age   new

PLANTING   *Photographed 6 September*
A display of summer succulents planted out in spring.
Position   sunny terrace
Compost   2:1 mixture of loam-based compost and grit
Fertilizer   none

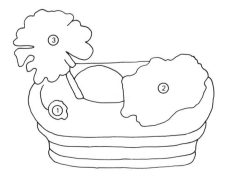

Key to plants
1.   1 red-leafed sempervivum
2.   1 green-leafed sempervivum
3.   *Aeonium arboreum* 'Atropurpureum'

Photograph on page 77

POT   Height 10 inches, width 16½ inches

Origin   Whichford (501)
Age   new

PLANTING   *Photographed 6 September*
A summer display of tender bedding planted out in May.
Position   full sun
Compost   multi-purpose peat-based compost
Fertilizer   a liquid tomato feed applied once a fortnight between May and September

Plants
1 ornamental cabbage
1 *Impatiens* (busy lizzie)

Photograph on page 78

POT – left	**POT** – right
Height 13 inches	8 inches
Width 19 inches	10½ inches
Origin	
Whichford (2005)	Whichford
Age	
new	new

PLANTING   *Photographed 6 September*
Each pot is planted with a single specimen for permanent pleasure.
Position   among cobbles in full sun
Compost   1:1 mixture of loam-based and multi-purpose peat-based composts
Fertilizer   a general-purpose liquid feed applied once a fortnight between May and September

Plants
Pot – left
Acer palmatum 'Dissectum'

Pot – right
Furcraea (needs winter protection)

Photograph on page 79

POTS AND PLANTS   *Photographed 6 September*

A display of summer foliage planted out in late May.
Position   sunny steps
Compost   1:1 mixture of loam-based and multi-purpose peat-based composts
Fertilizer   general-purpose liquid feed applied once a fortnight between May and September

POT A   *Height 8 inches, width 10½ inches*

Origin   Whichford
Age   new
Plant   *Furcraea* (needs protection in winter)

POT B   Height 20 inches, width 17½ inches

Origin   Whichford (604)
Age   new

Plants
1 trailing fuchsia
1 *Helichrysum petiolare*

POT C   Height 4½ inches, width 5 inches

Origin   Whichford (335)
Age   new
Plant   *Echeveria*

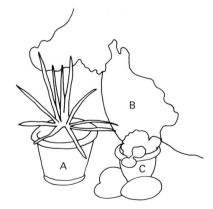

TINTINHULL HOUSE
Pages 80–83

Penelope Hobhouse

Penelope Hobhouse buys in a standard loam-based compost for her pots as she has no equipment to sterilize loam herself. She has experimented with a new super-absorbant gel. A very small amount mixed with the compost holds a great volume of water, each piece of gel releasing water slowly as the surrounding compost dries out. The effects are of great benefit in hot weather.

A balanced liquid feed is applied once a fortnight during the growing season.

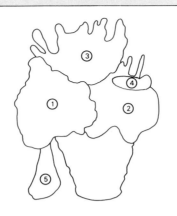

Photograph on page 80

POTS AND PLANTS *Photographed 26 June*

Each pot is planted simply for summer display.

Position   sunny

POT A   Height 13½ inches, width 15 inches

Origin   traditional seakale forcer
Age   at least 50 years
Plant   *Bidens polyepsis*

POT B – see below and page 82

POT C   Height 5 inches, width 10 inches

Origin   traditional English
Age   at least 50 years
Plant   sedum

POT D   Height 13 inches, width 13 inches

Origin   Italian
Age   10 years
Plant   heliotrope

POT E   Height 12½ inches, width 19 inches

Origin   Whichford (905)
Age   new

Plants

Helichrysum petiolare
Verbena peruviana var. *alba*

POT F   Height 6 inches, width 12 inches

Origin   Whichford (2021)
Age   new

Photograph on page 82

POT   Height 14 inches, width 18 inches

Origin   Impruneta
Age   new

PLANTING   *Photographed 26 June*

Tender summer bedding planted out in late spring.
Position   sunny

Key to plants

1. *Helichrysum petiolare*
2. *Helichrysum italicum* var. *microphyllum*
3. *Arisodontea capensis*
4. *Nemesia umbonata*
5. *Sphaeralcea munroana*

BOURTON HOUSE
Pages 84–91

Mr and Mrs Paice

Paul Williams, the resident gardener, always uses a loam-based compost in all the containers. The weight helps to stablize the pots and prevents them from blowing over, and it is easier to wet than peat if it dries out in hot weather. It also retains nutrients well; these are electro-magnetically attracted to the fine clay particles in the soil and therefore less easily leached out by watering, a problem with peat-based composts which contain no loam.

A slow-release fertilizer, richer in phosphates and potassium than nitrogen, is mixed in to the compost before planting to further combat the problem of nutrient loss. This encourages flowering, and gives a good green foliage.

A solution of sulphate of ammonia is applied frequently during the growing season. This must not be overdone, or the excess nitrogen may cause foliage to proliferate at the expense of flowering display. A little slow-release fertilizer may also be worked into the surface compost midway through the season to give the plants an extra boost.

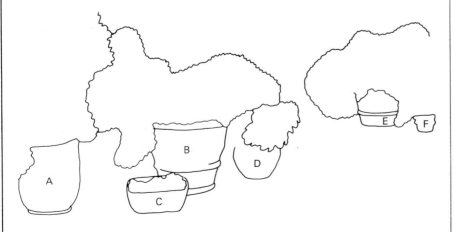

Photograph on page 86

POT   Height 7 inches, width 8 inches

Origin   Tony Murphy of Middle Barton Pottery

Age 8 years

PLANTING   *Photographed 2 August*
A summer display of tender perennials. It was found that there were too many plants for a pot of this size as, even in the shade, this grouping was forever drying out. Planted out at the end of May.

Position   in shade, but doesn't need to be

Key to plants

1. 1 *Glechoma hederacea* 'Variegata'
2. 2 *Tropaeolum nanum* 'Peach Melba'
3. 1 *Pelargonium fragrans* 'Variegatum'
4. 1 yellow *Begonia* x *tuberhybrida*
5. 1 *Verbena peruviana* var. *alba*

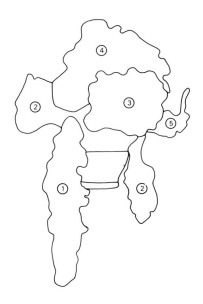

Photograph on page 87

POT   Height 32½ inches, width 12 inches

Origin   traditional English
Age 50 years or more

PLANTING   *Photographed 2 August*
A summer display of tender perennials planted out at the end of May.
Position   sunny with afternoon shade

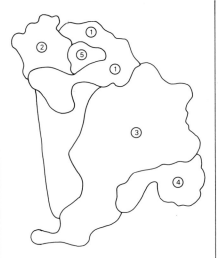

Key to plants

1. 2 *Cuphea signata*
2. 1 rosy red pelargonium
3. 2 *Bidens ferulifolia*
4. 2 red pelargonium
5. 1 *Tropaeolum majus* 'Hermine Gnashof'

Photograph on page 88

POT   Height 10 inches, width 10 inches

Origin   traditional English
Age 50 years or more

PLANTING   *Photographed 2 August*
Two identical pots planted with tender perennials and annuals for summer display, planted out at the end of May.
Position   light shade

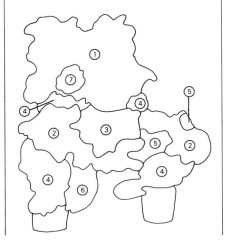

Key to plants

1. 1 *Abutilon* 'Canary Bird'
2. 5 *Petunia* 'Brass Band'
3. 3 *Plectranthus coleoides* 'Marginatus'
4. 8 apricot pansies
5. 2 *Nemesia caerulea*
6. 1 *Tropaeolum nanum* 'Peach Melba'
7. 1 *Verbena peruviana* var. *alba*

Photograph on page 89 – bottom

POTS   Various traditional pots, all around 50 years old.

PLANTING   *Photographed 25 September*
A mixture of tender and foliage plants, some brought straight out of the greenhouse, to combine contrasting colours, textures and forms. Planted out at the end of May.
Position   sheltered; sunny in the mornings and shady in the afternoons

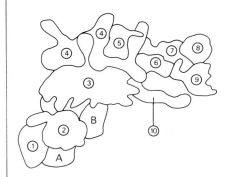

Key to plants

1. *Ophiopogon planiscapus* var. *nigrescens*
2. *Echeveria*
3. *Hosta* 'Thomas Hogg' (*H. undulata* 'Albomarginata')
4. *Helichrysum bracteatum* 'Dargan Hill Monarch'
5. *Melianthus major*
6. *Cuphea signata* 'Variegata'
7. *Lampranthus* (shrubby mesembryanthemum)
8. red pelargonium
9. *Argyranthemum foeniculaceum* pink form
10. *Gazania krebsiana*

Photograph on page 90

	POT A	POT B
Height	7 inches	11 inches
Width	16½ inches	20 inches

Origin

Whichford	Whichford
(plain 1420)	(1218)

Age

3 years	2 years

PLANTING   *Photographed 2 August*

A summer display of tender perennials planted out at the end of May.

Position   sunny

Key to plants

Pot A

1. 3 *Ophiopogon planiscapus* var. *nigrescens*
2. 1 *Begonia rex*

Pot B

1. 1 *Phormium* 'Purpureum'
2. 3 *Argyranthemum frutescens* 'Jamaica Primrose'
3. 3 *Cuphea signata* 'Variegata'
4. 3 *Gazania* 'Cream Beauty'

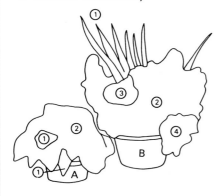

Photograph on page 91

	POT A	POT B
Height	10 inches	26 inches
Width	10 inches	9 inches (base),
		19 inches (top)

Origin   traditional English

Age   50 years or more

PLANTING   *Photographed 2 August*

A summer display of tender shrubs and perennials planted out in early June.

Position   shade, where they thrived

Key to plants

1. 4 red pelargoniums
2. 1 *Kalanchoe* 'Tessa'
3. 1 *Fuchsia santa-rosae*
4. 2 *Tropaeolum majus* 'Hermine Gnashof'
5. 1 yellow pendulous *Begonia* x *tuberhybrida*
6. 1 *Helichrysum petiolare* 'Limelight'
7. 1 *Fuchsia* 'Traudchen Bonstedt'

BARNSLEY HOUSE   *Pages 92–99*

Rosemary Verey

Rosemary Verey always mixes up her own potting compost. The special ingredient is supplied by her bantams, for the loam used comes from inside their pecking run, which is moved anually. This loam is rich in nitrogen, and is combined with an equal amount of peat. To this is added perlite, one eighth part by volume, to aid moisture retention.

Photograph on page 92

POT   Height 6½ inches, width 14 inches

Origin   Whichford (421D)

Age   new

PLANTING   *Photographed 25 July*

A summer display of tender perennials planted out at the very end of April.

Position   a warm sunny corner

Key to plants

1. 1 *Osteospermum* cv.
2. 3 *Helichrysum petiolare* 'Variegatum'
3. 2 *Verbena peruviana* var. *alba*
4. 1 *Pelargonium* 'Lady Plymouth'

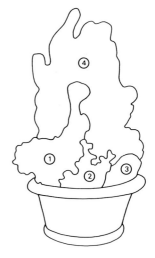

Photograph on page 95 – top

POT   Height 9½ inches, width 10 inches

Origin   English
Age   20 years or more

PLANTING   *Photographed 25 July*
Permanent, for summer display. Planted out in autumn 1987.
Position   sunny; moved indoors or into the greenhouse over winter

Plant   *Fuchsia* 'Checkerboard' (trained as a standard)

Photograph on page 96

POT   Height 19½ inches, width 27 inches

Origin   Whichford (907)
Age   new

PLANTING   *Photographed 25 July*
A mixed summer display planted out at the beginning of May.
Position   sunny corner of sheltered courtyard

Key to plants
1.   1 *Lavandula spica*
2.   1 *Coprosam repens* 'Marble Queen' (staked to make a weeping standard)
3.   1 *Argyranthemum frutescens* 'Jamaica Primrose'
4.   3 *Osteospermum* 'Langtrees'
5.   3 *Bidens ferulifolia*
6.   1 fern

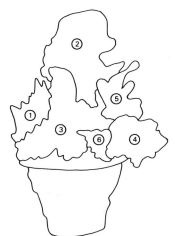

Photograph on page 97 – left

POT   Height 8½ inches, width 12 inches

Origin   Whichford (1330)
Age   new

PLANTING   *Photographed 25 June*
All-the-year-round display planted up in 1987.
Position   in sun outdoors in summer, frost-proof place in winter.

Plants   4 *Echeveria gibbiflora* 'Metallica'

Photograph on page 97 – right

POT   Height 13 inches, width 18 inches

Origin   Italy
Age   15 years

PLANTING   *Photographed 25 July*
Permanent, for winter display; originally planted out in winter.
Position   south-facing veranda

Plant   1 *Buxus sempervirens*

Photograph on page 98 – top

POT A	**POT B**
Height 10 inches	21 inches
Width 12 inches	19 inches
Origin	
Crete	Clive Bowen of Shebbear Pottery
Age	
new	new

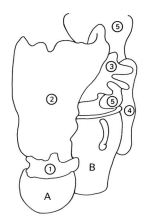

PLANTING   *Photographed 25 July*
A summer display of shrubs and annuals planted out at the beginning of May.
Position   sunny

Key to plants
1.   6 *Lobelia* 'Kathleen Mallard'
2.   1 double pink fuchsia
3.   1 *Cotoneaster horizontalis* 'Variegatus'
4.   1 *Fuchsia* 'Thalia'
5.   4 *Ipomoea hederacea*

Photograph on page 99 – bottom

POTS AND PLANTS *Photographed 25 June*
A contrasting group of perennials and succulents displayed on a stone table.

POT A   Height 5 inches, width 7 inches

Origin   David Garland
Age   5 years
Planted up   spring

POT B   Height 4 inches, width 9 inches

Origin   David Garland
Age   5 years
Planted up   1985

POT C   Height 3½ inches, width 10½ inches

Origin   traditional English
Age   50 years

Key to plants
1.   dianthus
2. and 3.   saxifrages
4.   *Echeveria gibbiflora* 'Metallica'
5.   *Gazania* cream

SUNNYSIDE FARM *Pages 100–105*

Jim Keeling

I always use a strong loam-based potting compost (John Innes No. 3) for all my container-grown plants. This provides plenty of nutrients for shrubs and perennials to keep them going for two or three years if necessary, although I tend to repot more frequently. Once a week during the growing season I apply an all-purpose soluble plant food which is taken in through the foliage as well as the roots. This keeps all the plants growing well and looking perky.

Photograph on page 101

POT   Height 11½ inches, width 24 inches

Origin   Whichford (2024)
Age   3 years

PLANTING   *Photographed 26 July*
Summer display of plants with aromatic foliage, planted out in late spring.
Position   sunny

Key to plants
1. 1 *Salvia officinalis* 'Purpurascens'
2. 2 *Pelargonium* 'Lady Plymouth' (grey form)
3. 1 *Pelargonium graveolens*

Photograph on page 102–103

POTS AND PLANTS   *Photographed 26 July*
An arrangement of pots for permanent display.

POT A   Height 4¾ inches, width 4 inches

Origin   Whichford (1242)
Age   4 years
Plants   oxalis (left) and sempervivum (right)

POT B   Height 7½ inches, width 7 inches

Origin   Whichford (1244)
Age   4 years
Plant   *Thymus vulgaris*

POT C   Height 13 inches, width 18 inches

Origin   Whichford (834)
Age   2 years
Plant   *Rosa* 'Gertrude Jekyll' (shrub rose)

POT D   Height 12½ inches, width 19 inches

Origin   Whichford (905)
Age   4 years
Plant   *Mespilus germanica* (medlar tree)

Photograph on page 104

POT   Height 7 inches, width 9½ inches

Origin   Whichford (016)
Age   4 years

PLANTING   *Photographed 26 July*
A permanent planting in its first year.
Position   frost-free, otherwise will need some protection during the winter months

Plant   *Pelargonium tricolor* hybrid

Photograph on page 105 – bottom

POT – left	**POT** – right
Height 43 inches	11 inches
Width 24 inches	15½ inches
Origin	
Whichford	Whichford
(Sassanian jar)	(621E)
Age	
new	2 years

PLANTING   *Photographed 26 May*
Permanent and evergreen, repotted annually in spring.
Position   protected in winter to avoid frost damage
Plants
Soleirolia soleirolii (left)
Buxus sempervirens (right)

Photograph on page 105 – top

POTS AND PLANTS   *Photographed 26 July*
An arrangement of pots, elephants and plants with silver foliage.

POT A   Height 13 inches, width 19 inches

Origin   Whichford (0021)
Age   2 years
Plant
Helichrysum italicum

POT B   Height 13 inches, width 14 inches

Origin   Whichford (502B)
Age   2 years

POT C   Height 18 inches, width 14 inches

Origin   Whichford (2050)
Age   2 years
Plants
1 *Helichrysum italicum*
1 *Senecio* 'Sunshine'

POT D   Height 6 inches, width 10 inches

Origin   Whichford (802)
Age   4 years

POT E   Height 4½ inches, width 5 inches

Origin   Whichford (334)

POT F   Height 4 inches, width 7½ inches

Origin   Whichford (1211)

Age   4 years

POT G   Height 7 inches, width 8 inches

Origin   Whichford (336)

Age   4 years

POT H   Height 4¾ inches, width 4 inches

Origin   Whichford (1242)

Age   4 years

GOTHIC HOUSE   *Pages 106–111*

Andrew Lawson

Andrew admits that his plantings are "pot-luck" with anything going in, preferably with flowers of white or pink. He makes up his own potting compost, using peat, well-rotted garden compost and the loam from turves which have been stacked until they crumble.

During the growing season he feeds his plants once a week with an all-purpose liquid fertilizer.

Photograph on page 106

POT   Height 10 inches, width 19 inches

Origin   Devon

Age   100 years or more

PLANTING   *Photographed 24 July*

Summer flower and foliage set out in late spring.

Position   sunny

Key to plants

1. 1 *Cosmos* 'Sensation'
2. 4 white petunias
3. 3 *Agapanthus* Headbourne Hybrids (in adjacent pot)

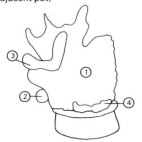

Photograph on page 110

POTS AND PLANTS *Photographed 30 June*

A mixed display of mainly tender plants in a range of traditional pots including Devon "trendles". The larger pots were planted out in early May; the smaller pots, permanently planted and overwintered indoors, were brought outside early in May.

Position   sunny terrace during summer

Key to plants

1. *Nicotinana affinis* (self-seeded, the pot also contained tulip bulbs for spring colour)
2. *Pelargonium peltatum* 'Album'
3. *Lilium regale* (moved indoors for winter)
4. *Pelargonium graveolens* (moved indoors for winter)
5. *Pelargonium fragrans* (moved indoors for winter)
6. *Fuchsia* 'Hawkshead'

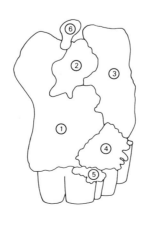

Photograph on page 111

POT   Height 7 inches, width 5 inches

Origin   unknown

Age   about 3 years

PLANTING   *Photographed 30 June*

A herb pot planted up in spring.

Position   near kitchen door

Key to plants

1. mint (*Mentha spicata*)
2. parsley (*Petroselium crispum*)
3. chives (*Allium schoenoprasum*)

CHILCOMBE HOUSE *Pages 112–17*
John Hubbard

At Chilcombe House a peat-based compost is used in the containers, supplemented during the summer months with a balanced organic fertilizer applied as a liquid feed every fortnight.

Photograph on pages 114–15

POT Height 11 inches, width 13½ inches

Origin Whichford (621E)
Age new

PLANTING *Photographed 27 June*
Tender perennials and pansies which will provide a show from early summer into autumn. These were planted out in late spring.
Position against a south-facing wall

Key to plants
1. 2 *Felicia amelloides*
2. 3 yellow and black pansies
3. 2 *Helichrysum petiolare*
4. 1 *Salvia guaranitica*
5. 1 *Salvia cacliifolia*

Photograph on page 116

POT Height 15 inches, width 21 inches

Origin Whichford (621C)
Age new

PLANTING *Photographed 27 June*
Summer flowers and foliage, planted out in late spring.
Position full sun

Key to plants
1. 3 *Calendula officinalis*
2. 1 *Heuchera micrantha* 'Palace Purple'
3. 3 *Tropaeolum majus* (orange and red flowers)

Photograph on page 117 – top

POT Height 8 inches, width 9 inches

Origin traditional English
Age 50 years or more

PLANTING *Photographed 27 June*
Permanently planted pots for summer display set out in early spring.
Position against a south-facing wall

Plants
7 *Lilium regale*
5 *Foeniculum vulgare* var. *purpureum* (purple fennel)

Photograph on page 117 – bottom

POT Height 11 inches, width 15½ inches

Origin Whichford (621E)
Age new

PLANTING *Photographed 27 July*
These tender perennials were planted out in late spring and will flower all summer long.
Position full sun

Key to plants
1. 1 *Verbena* 'Sissinghurst'
2. 1 *Verbena* 'Silver Ann'
3. 1 *Sphaeralcea miniata*

CASTLE ASHBY *Pages 118–21, 133*
Joanne Miles

At Castle Ashby a peat-based compost is used, mixed by hand. This contains an organic, phosphate-rich fertilizer to encourage healthy, vigorous growth in all the potted plants.

Photograph on page 118

POTS AND PLANTS *Photographed 21 September*
A permanent display of foliage positioned to block entry to the pond in the conservatory. These pots were planted up in summer 1986. Each spring, after some of the old surface compost has been scratched away, a top dressing of fresh compost is applied.

POT A Height 12 inches, width 11 inches

Origin traditional
Age 50 years or more
Plant *Arundinaria viridistriata*

POT B Height 16 inches, width 17 inches

Origin traditional
Age 50 years or more
Plant *Cyperus papyrus*

POT C Height 16 inches, width 17 inches

Origin traditional (stamped Conway Cawne Lim. Royal Potteries, Weston-super-Mare)
Age 50 years or more
Plant *Sinarundinaria (Arundinaria) nitida*

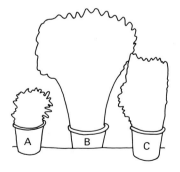

Photograph on page 121 – bottom

POT Height 16 inches, width 19 inches

Origin England
Age nineteenth century

PLANTING *Photographed 21 September*
Summer display in the conservatory planted up during the summer of 1986.

Position sunny conservatory. Brought into a heated greenhouse at the end of October for the winter, although it did survive one winter in the unheated conservatory.
Fertilizer liquid feed applied once a fortnight
Plant *Begonia haageana*

Photograph on page 133

POT Height 28 inches, width 21 inches

Origin J. M. Blashfield
Age about 120 years

PLANTING *Photographed 21 September*
Tender perennials for summer flower and foliage underplanted with *Tulipa* 'Red Emperor' and *Myosotis palustris* (forget-me-nots) for spring display. A groundcover of *Vinca major* 'Variegata' underplanted with 300 bulbs of *Tulipa* 'Purissima' surrounds the urn.

Summer display planted out late spring
Spring display planted out autumn
Position semi-shade

Plants
3 *Helichrysum petiolare*
3 scarlet pelargoniums
1 *Pelargonium* 'Sybil Holmes'

SOUTHVIEW   *Pages 122–29, 130, 134*
Rupert Golby

To grow plants well in pots, they must never dry out. So it is for its ability to hold water that Rupert Golby chooses a multi-purpose peat-based compost. During the growing season he applies an all-purpose soluble plant food and an organic liquid feed based on seaweed once a week to keep his displays flourishing.

Photograph on page 122

POT Height 26 inches, width 24 inches

Origin Whichford (2001)
Age new, but "aged" with a lime-wash

PLANTING *Photographed 25 September*
A large mixed display of summer-flowering tender perennials and fuchsias planted out in late May.
Position sunny terrace

Key to plants
1. 1 *Phormium* 'Bronze Baby'
2. 1 *Fuchsia magellanica* 'Versicolor'
3. 1 *Verbena* 'Sissinghurst'
4. 1 *Sphaeralcea munroana*
5. 1 *Diascia* 'Rupert Lambert'
6. 3 *Pelargonium* 'Scarlet Unique'
7. 1 *Fuchsia* 'Thalia'

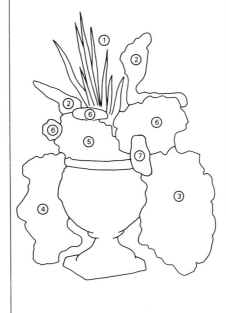

Photograph on pages 124–25

POTS Height 20 inches, width 30 inches

Origin Impruneta
Age new

PLANTING *Photographed 25 July*
A mixed summer planting of bedding plants and tender perennials planted out in late May.
Position south-facing open terrace

Key to planting
POT A
1. 2 *Helichrysum petiolare*
2. 4 *Petunia* 'White Cloud'
3. 1 *Argyranthemum foeniculaceum*
4. 2 *Felicia amelloides* 'Santa Anita'
5. 2 *Pelargonium* 'Lady Plymouth'
6. 1 *Melianthus major*
7. 1 *Verbena* 'Loveliness'

POT B
1. 2 *Verbena* 'Loveliness'
2. 1 *Melianthus major*
3. 2 *Verbena tennera*
4. 3 *Petunia* 'White Cloud'
5. 1 *Argyranthemum foeniculaceum*
6. 1 *Plectostachys serpyllifolia*
7. 1 *Nepeta*

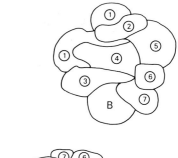

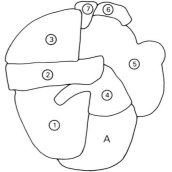

Photograph on page 126

POT Height 22 inches, width 19 inches

Origin Impruneta
Age 7 years

PLANTING *Photographed 25 July*
A summer display of tender perennials in pinks and whites planted out in late spring.
Position sunny

Key to plants
1. 1 *Argyranthemum foeniculaceum*
2. 2 *Verbena* 'Silver Ann'
3. 1 *Diascia rigescens*
4. 1 *Tanacetum ptarmiciflorum* (*Pyrethrum ptarmicifolium*)
5. 2 *Plectostachys serpyllifolia*

Photograph on page 128 – top

POT Height 9¼ inches, width 12 inches

Origin Whichford (1207)
Age 1 year

PLANTING *Photographed 25 August*
A summer planting of tender perennials, and petunias in three identical pots set out in late May.
Position a south-facing wall

Key to plants
1. 4 *Pelargonium* 'Paul Crampel'
2. 1 *Verbena chamaedrifolia*
3. 1 *Cosmos atrosanguineus*
4. 1 *Petunia* 'Red Joy'

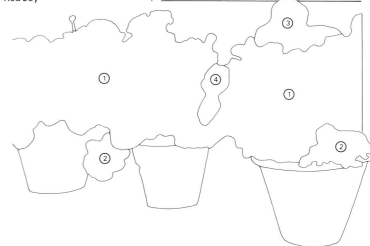

Photograph on page 128 – bottom

POT Height 20 inches, width 30 inches

Origin Impruneta
Age new

PLANTING *Photographed 5 May*
A simple but elegant bedding display for late winter and spring, each pot identically planted up in late October.
Position sunny south-facing terrace

Plants
20 *Tulipa* 'White Triumphator'
10 pansies, 'Senator Celestial Blue'

Photograph on page 127

TROUGH Height 15 inches, width 10 inches, 45 inches long

Origin Impruneta
Age 7 years

PLANTING *Photographed 25 July*
Massed display of tender perennials and bedding plants chosen for their fine texture of flower and foliage. Planted out in late spring.
Position sunny

Key to plants
1. 2 *Diascia vigilis*
2. 2 *Argyranthemum foeniculaceum* Picnic form
3. 2 x *Linaria* x *Diascia*
4. 4 *Diascia* 'Ruby Field'
5. 3 *Argyranthemum* 'Vancouver'
6. 2 *Leucanthemum gayanum*
7. 1 *Verbena* 'Sissinghurst'

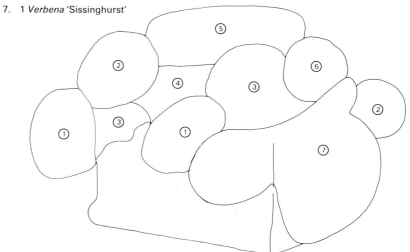

Photograph on page 129

POT   Height 29 inches, width 36 inches

Origin Impruneta
Age 7 years

PLANTING   *Photographed 25 July*
A mixture of permanent and temporary plants create a study in green and white. Planted out in May.
Position south-west-facing corner

Key to plants
1. 1 *Aralia elata* 'Variegata'
2. 3 *Argyranthemum foeniculaceum* 'Chelsea Girl'
3. 3 *Verbena peruviana* var. *alba*
4. 2 *Pelargonium* 'Lady Plymouth'

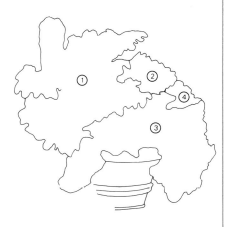

Photograph on page 134

POT   Height 29 inches, width 39 inches

Origin Whichford (2010)
Age 2 years

PLANTING   *Photographed 2 September*
Mixed display of tender perennials and purple sage planted out in late May.
Position sunny south-facing terrace

Key to plants
1. 1 *Penstemon* 'Sour Grapes'
2. 1 *Salvia officinalis* 'Purpurascens'
3. 2 *Felicia amelloides* 'Santa Anita'

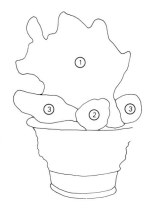

Photograph on page 130

POT   Height 8 inches, width 9 inches

Origin Peter Strong
Age 3 years

PLANTING   *Photographed 25 July*
A simple planting of yellow-flowering tender perennials selected to harmonize with the golden leaved hop (*Humulus lupulus* 'Aureus') growing up the wall. Planted out in May.
Position morning sun

Key to plants
1. 1 *Bidens aurea*
2. 1 *Argyranthemum maderense*

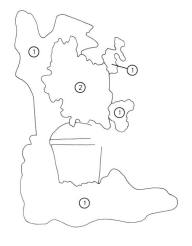

APPENDIX

PEOPLE AND POTTERIES

ALBERTI, Leon Battista (1404-72)
The influence of this great Florentine humanist on garden design derives chiefly from his treatise *De re aedificatoria libri X* ('Ten Books on Architecture') of 1452. These were much studied by his patrons, who included members of the Medici and Este families.

ARCHIMEDES (c. 287-212 BC)
The greatest mathematician of antiquity. He was born in Syracuse and was a friend of King Hieron II.

ASHBEE, Charles Robert (1836-1942)
Influential designer, writer and principal organizer of the Arts and Crafts Movement. He founded the Guild and School of Handicraft in 1888 in the East End of London. In 1902 he moved out to Chipping Camden in the Cotswolds to create the School of Arts and Crafts, which promoted craft skills and husbandry. Despite international successes, he began to lose faith in handicrafts and in 1910 stated that "modern civilization rests on machinery". In 1915 he gave up all association with crafts and went to teach English at Cairo University.

BLASHFIELD, John Marriott (1811-82)
Originally a manufacturer of scagliola and cement in Southwark, south of London. In 1851 Blashfield acquired moulds from Coade's factory and started to produce architectural terracotta and statuary. In 1858 he moved to Lincolnshire, and later founded the Stamford Terra Cotta Company which went bankrupt in 1875.

BROWN, Lancelot "Capability" (1716-83)
English landscape designer who transformed the grounds of an extraordinary number of the great houses of the eighteenth century. He designed on a grand scale, redirecting rivers, flooding valleys, moving hillsides and abolishing all traces of formality.

CARDEW, Michael (1901-83)
An English studio potter, and early student of Bernard Leach. Unlike Leach, he turned to the English tradition for inspiration, specializing in lead-glazed slipware for everyday use at Winchcombe Pottery, Gloucestershire. In 1942 he went to West Africa, where he produced pottery that combined European techniques with African traditions. On his return to England, he founded Wenford Bridge Pottery in Cornwall.

CAUS, Salomon de (c.1576-1626)
French Huguenot engineer and garden designer, he was at the English court from 1610-13. He published several books including *Les Raisons des forces mouvantes* (1615) which set out the principles of hydraulics.

CAXTON, William (c.1422-91)
The first English printer, also influential translator and publisher.

"COUNTRY" POTTERIES
Small craft potteries in which local clays were made into useful earthenware vessels for the surrounding communities.

DOULTON POTTERY AND PORCELAIN COMPANY (DOULTON)
Established by John Doulton in 1815, the pottery began by specializing in functional stoneware, but later became celebrated for its varied "artistic" products.

FIENNES, Celia (1662-1741)
Englishwoman known for the travels and the descriptions of gardens she recorded in her journal between 1685 and c. 1712.

JEKYLL, Gertrude (1843-1932)
English garden designer and writer. She brought an eye for colour and a love for English rural tradition, including that of the cottage garden, to the gardens she made. She often worked with her friend and partner, the architect Sir Edwin Lutyens, who shared her understanding and deep interest in traditional crafts and materials.

LONDON, George (d. 1714)
Pupil of John Rose and last of the great formal garden designers, he played a leading part in the gardens of Longleat House, Chatsworth, and Castle Howard. His nursery at Brompton Park, run for many years in partnership with Henry Wise, enjoyed great renown.

LOUDON, John Claudius (1783-1843)
A Scot of remarkable energy, Loudon made a fortune in farming before retiring to devote himself to gardens and garden writing. His books, encyclopaedias and magazines were essential reference works in their day, and exerted considerable influence on the rise of the suburban garden. His wife, Jane (1807-58), helped him in his work and wrote on gardening, botany and other subjects.

MEDICI, Cosimo di (1389-1464)
Known as Cosimo the Elder, he was the wealthiest man of his time, with banks in all the great cities of Europe. Patron of artists and architects, he was one of the first to commission "Renaissance" garden designs. He recreated Plato's Academy at the Villa Medici in Careggi under the humanist Marsilio Ficino. His love of learning led to his methodical research throughout Christendom and the East, with Sultan Mehmed II's permission, for ancient manuscripts for what was to become the Laurentian Library in Florence.

MORRIS, William (1834-96)
Leading figure in late Victorian decorative arts: craftsman, designer, poet and political theorist. Morris started a "firm for producing decorative articles" in 1861 which produced handmade wallpapers, carpets and textiles, creating designs still popular today. He believed that "real art" can only be made "by the people and for the people as a happiness for the maker and user", and dreamt of a future without machines where the mediaeval guild system would be restored.

MINTON'S POTTERY AND PORCELAIN FACTORY (MINTON)
This pottery was founded at Stoke-on-Trent in 1796 by Thomas Minton, reputed inventor of the Willow Pattern design which still flourishes today.

PLINY THE YOUNGER (c. 61-112)
Roman statesman who published nine books of literary letters, two of which describe the gardens of two of his villas, one near Rome and the other in Tuscany. He was nephew and adopted son of Pliny the Elder.

ROBBIA, Luca della (1400-82)
Italian sculptor best known for his glazed terracotta reliefs. His business was carried on by his nephew, Andrea della Robbia (1435-1525), and subsequently his sons, until well into the sixteenth century.

ROSE, John (1629-77)
Studied under the French gardener Le Nôtre, and brought his style of design to England. Unfortunately little of his own work survives. He

was also a brilliant horticulturist and specialist in fruit growing.

ROUSSEAU, Jean Jacques (1712-78)
Philosopher and political theorist whose treatises and novels inspired the Romantics and the leaders of the French revolution. In *La Nouvelle Héloïse* (1761) Rousseau wrote that gardens should be "natural" and intimate in nature.

SWITZER, Stephen (1682-1745)
Better known for his writings than his garden design, his major work was the three volume *Ichnographia Rustica* of 1718. Early in his life, he worked with George London and Henry Wise. His own designs were influenced by his theory that whole estates should be designed round one or two axial lines in the grand manner. In later life he set up as a seedsman.

THEOPHRASTUS (c. 370-286 BC)
Greek philosopher and botanist, he was a pupil of Plato and then of Aristotle, whom he succeeded at the Lyceum, where the garden and walk were a place of study. He wrote the *Enquiry into Plants*, which contains the first systematic classification of plants in Western literature.

TRADESCANT, John the elder
(c. 1570-1638)
Plant collector and gardener, responsible for the introduction of many plants to Britain. He had a succession of powerful patrons, including Charles I. While working for the Earl of Salisbury, he visited Holland, Flanders and France collecting trees and flowers for Hatfield. Later he went to Russia and North Africa, and became a member of the Virginia Company, introducing several North American plants. He and his son, John the younger, (1608-62), who continued his work, had a garden at Lambeth for their rarities.

VASARI, Giorgio (1511-74)
A prolific and successful Italian painter and architect, he remains best-known for his *Lives of the Artists*, first published in 1550 and in a revised and enlarged edition in 1568.

WISE, Henry (1653-1738)
Garden designer and partner to George London at Brompton Park Nurseries in Kensington, with whom he planned and planted gardens all over England. In 1700, it was agreed that Wise should concentrate on royal parks and gardens, while London rode about the country advising estate owners. In 1702, Wise became Master Gardener to Queen Anne.

WYATT, Sir Matthew Digby
(1820-1877)
Architect and administrator who published many books and papers on the decorative arts. He worked with Isambard Kingdom Brunel designing architectural details for Paddington and Bristol Meads stations, and on parts of the Foreign Office in Whitehall, London. As Secretary, he was actively involved in the Great Exhibition of 1851, and in 1869 became the first Slade Professor of Fine Art at Cambridge.

TECHNICAL TERMS

BALL CLAY
A type of high-firing clay, usually very plastic, and firing to a white or buff colour.

BISCUIT
Once-fired ware which is ready to be glazed.

FLASHING
When a pot is licked by the flame in a kiln it sometimes changes colour, or is "flashed". This happens if the flame is oxygen hungry, when it will take oxygen from the pot. In such a case the terracotta will change from red to black or grey.

KNOT
A term coined in the late fifteenth century to describe a twisted pattern created out of clipped evergreen plants such as box or rosemary. The areas in between were planted with flowers or left as bare earth which was sometimes coloured with pigment. To be fully appreciated the design needed to be viewed from above. During the seventeenth century as designs became increasingly elaborate, pattern books were published.

LUTING
To join two pieces of clay together. If the clay is too wet, it is difficult to handle neatly, and if too dry the pieces will crack apart as they finish drying. Ideally, the clay is a damp leather-hard, or "green", and the surfaces to be joined are stuck together with a little water or slip after first having been roughened.

LOGGIA
A gallery, room or arcade open on one side.

PLEACH, PLEACHED
Derived from the French "to braid". Woody plants such as lime or hornbeam can be trained along a frame to form a dense arbour, tunnel or screen. These must be pruned hard each winter during the formative years when natural grafting may occur where branches of adjacent plants cross or are tied together.

POTAGER
A sixteenth-century French term describing knot gardens where vegetables were planted between the clipped ever greens. It came to be more generally applied to formal kitchen gardens where plants are laid out in patterns. The restored garden at Villandry is probably the best-known example of a potager.

PARTERRE
In sixteenth-century France this referred to a garden where flowers were arranged in beds. Later it was used to describe rectangular beds laid out in patterns with knots, and pools integrated into the design. As with knots, the patterns became increasingly complex culminating in the *parterres de broideries* of seventeenth-century France. In the eighteenth century parterres became fashionable in North America; the restored water parterre at Dumbarton Oaks is an outstanding example.

SLIP
Clay mixed with water to the consistency of cream.

SLIPWARE
A kind of earthenware decorated with different coloured slips.

SWAGS
Looped garlands of fruit, foliage and flowers, often used as a design motif by the Etruscans and the Romans to decorate sarcophagi.

TUFA
An extremely porous limestone rock much used in association with alpine plants. The roots of such plants grow down into the soft rock and benefit from the excellent drainage it provides.

LIST OF SUPPLIERS

GREAT BRITAIN

Whichford Pottery
(producer)
Whichford, Shipston on Stour,
Warwickshire CV36 5PG
Tel: 0608 84416

The author's own pottery, and biggest producer of handmade terracotta flowerpots in the British Isles. Over one hundred and fifty lines to choose from, including Baroque urns and a full range of horticultural ware. Exported all over the world. Colour brochure available.

There are many small English producers of flowerpots. I mention here a few that I know personally.

Clive Bowen (producer)
Shebbear Pottery, Beaworthy,
Devon EX21 8QZ
The best modern exponent of the Devon slipware tradition, Clive also makes some flowerpots in his wood-fired kiln. All thrown, they range from wallpots to very large pieces.

Jonathan Garrett (producer)
Hare Lane Pottery, Cranborne,
nr Wimborne, Dorset BH21 5QT
Tel: 07254 700
Jonathan is a great perfectionist. He throws a standard range of pots supplemented by many one-offs, all at reasonable prices. The pots are often textured, and his wood-fired kiln gives them lively colourings.

Mark Griffiths (producer)
The Old School, Culmington,
nr Ludlow, Shropshire SY8 2DF
Mark uses a coarsely-textured clay from Ruabon to make strong, sturdy pots, including big pieces. A good range, often with round shapes and interesting colours from "flashing" in the kiln.

A. Harris & Sons (producer)
Pottery Lane, Wrecclesham,
Surrey GU10 4QJ
Tel: 0252 715318
Founded in 1872, now run by the fifth generation. Where the author trained. Still produces a good range of pots in traditional orange colour.

John Huggins (producer)
Courtyard Pottery, Cricklade Road,
Swindon, Wiltshire
Tel: 0793 72111
The "sun and rain", sprigged round the shoulder of a pot, are one of John's hallmarks. The pots are a darker red than some, and number both thrown and pressed pots, including face wallpots and sets of lions' feet to raise pots off the ground.

Peter Strong (producer)
Dales Pottery, Wetherigs, Clifton Dykes, Penrith, Cumbria
Tel: 0768 62946
Trained in the Country tradition at Soil Hill Pottery, Peter hand-throws a range of pots including traditional flowerpots. He also produces Victorian hand-pressed ware from original moulds and square fern pans.

Mark Titchener (producer)
Chediston Pottery, Chediston Green, Halesworth, Suffolk IP19 0BB
Tel: 098685 242
A small family pottery, producing distinctive garden pots, using a wood fired kiln.

Pots and Pithoi (importer)
Grange Farm, Turners Hill Road, Crawley Down, West Sussex
Tel: 0342 714793
Rosie and Robin Lloyd import a good selection of Cretan pots. Produced for them at the Workers' Cooperative in Thrapsano.

Rassells (importer)
80 Earls Court Road, London
W8 6EQ
Tel: 01-937 0481
Stockists since the 1950s for one of the best small family firms in Impruneta. A limited supply, but top quality and reasonably priced.

USA

The following sources import good quality handmade terracotta.

The Clapper Company
1121 Washington Street
West Newton, MA 02165

Compleat Garden
5405 Broadway, San Antonio,
Texas 78209
Tel: (512) 822 0444

Devonshire
6 North Madison Street, Middleburg,
Virginia 22117
Tel: (703) 687 5990
302 Thames Street, Newport,
Rhode Island 02840
Main Street, PO Box 1860, Bridgehampton, New York 11932

Erkins Studios
662 Thames Street
Newport, RI 02840

Gardener's Eden
PO Box 7307
San Francisco, CA 94120

Hollyhock
214 South Larchmont Boulevard,
Los Angeles, California 90004
Tel: (213) 931 3400

Smith & Hawken
25 Corte Madera, Mill Valley,
California 94941
Tel: (415) 383 4050

Valerie Bernard Eglit
1311-A Montana Avenue,
Santa Monica, California 90403
Tel: (213) 393 1099

CANADA

The Well Furnished Garden
5635 West Boulevard
Vancouver BC V6M3W7

ITALY

There are hundreds of good potteries in Italy. The two below I can recommend personally.

Massini & Figli
via Fornaci, Impruneta, Toscana

M.I.T.A.L.
via Fornaci, Impruneta, Toscana

PLANTS

There are many sources of tender perennials and bedding plants. Unusual varieties can be obtained from:

Gould Farm Nurseries
Frittenden, Cranbrook,
Kent TN17 2DT
Tel: (058080) 234

Hopley's Plants Ltd
High Street, Much Hadham,
Hertfordshire SG10 6BU
Tel: (0279 84) 2509

FURTHER READING

There is no definitive work on flowerpots. So far, they seem to have escaped academic interest, so it is only since my recent visits to the Ceramics Department at the Victoria and Albert Museum that they have started a section entitled "Flowerpots" in their card index.

For the domestic tradition in Britain, I found the following most useful:
Oxfordshire Potters by Nancy Stebbing, John Rhodes and Maureen Mellor (Oxfordshire Museums Services Publication No. 13 1980)
The English Country Pottery, its History and Techniques the standard work by Peter Brears. (David and Charles, Newton Abbott 1973).

A number of books on traditional crafts mention flowerpots in passing:
Made in England by Dorothy Hartley (Eyre Methuen Ltd, London and Edinburgh 1974)
Rural Crafts of England by K.S. Woods (E.P. Publishing Ltd, Wakefield 1975)
Traditional Craftsmen by J. Geraint-Jenkins (Routledge and Keegan Paul, London 1965 and 1978).

The dedicated and multi-lingual may care to look at the following:
An article on early flowerpots in the Dutch ceramics periodical *Vrienden van de Netherlandse Ceramiek*
The catalogue, in Italian, of the exhibition *La Civilta del Cotto – Arte della Terracotta Nell'area Fiorentina dal XV al XX Secolo* (Impruneta 1980).

Luca della Robbia is to be found in the standard surveys of Renaissance art as well as the following:
Lives of the Artists by Giorgio Vasari, trans. George Bull (Penguin Books, Harmondsworth 1965 and other editions)
Luca della Robbia by John Pope-Henessy, (Phaidon, Oxford 1980).

A good introduction to the Arts and Crafts Movement is:
The Simple Life in the Cotswolds by Fiona MacCarthy (Lund Humphries, London 1981).

An invaluable work for the history of flowerpots in gardening:
A History of Garden Art by Marie Luis Gothein (J.M. Dent and Sons Ltd, London and Toronto 1928).

Many interesting details of the early use of pots can be found in:
Medieval Gardens by Sir Frank Crisp (the illustrations) (first published over 70 years ago and reprinted by Hacker Art Books, New York 1979).

More recently, there are:
A History of Gardens and Gardening by Edward Hyams (J.M. Dent and Sons Ltd, London 1971)
The English Garden by Laurence Fleming and Alan Gore (Michael Joseph, London 1979)
Italian Gardens by Georgina Masson (Thames and Hudson, London 1961)
The Book of Garden Ornament by Peter Hunt (J.M. Dent and Sons Ltd, London 1974)
The Garden – A Celebration of One Thousand Years of British Gardening exhibition catalogue (Victoria and Albert Museum, London 1979)
The Gardens of Pompeii, Herculaneum and the Villas Destroyed by Vesuvius by Wilhelmina F. Jashemski (Carateas Bros, New York, 1979)
Early Nurserymen by John Harvey (Phillimore and Co. Ltd, London and Chichester 1974).

References of flowerpots and garden ornaments can be found in many of the old gardening books, especially by Victorian writers such as Shirley Hibberd, John Claudius and Jane Loudon, Samuel Beeton, and, later, William Robinson and Gertrude Jekyll.

Practical advice on propagation and potting up can be found in comprehensive guides such as:
The Reader's Digest New Illustrated Guide to Gardening ed. Roy Hay (Reader's Digest Association Limited, London 1987)
The Collingridge Illustrated Encyclopedia of Gardening by Arthur Hellyer (Collingridge Books, London 1976, 1982).

There are many books specifically for the container gardener which offer tips and ideas. Of these, I recommend:
The Contained Garden by Kenneth A. Beckett, David Carr and David Stevens (Windward/W.H. Smith and Son Ltd, Leicester 1982).

ACKNOWLEDGEMENTS

A book like this is a team effort and there are many people to be thanked: first, my contributors to Chapter 2, for their enthusiasm, support, and hard work with pots and plants, especially Andrew Lawson who also took the excellent photographs; Ian Jackson at Eddison Sadd, without whom the book would still be just a vague idea; Nicki Bennett, who acted as coordinator, researcher, co-interviewer, and who wrote the first drafts for Chapter 2; my secretary, Jane Lancia, who never baulked at the endless revisions in strange hieroglyphs; Mike Ricketts for design; Barbara Haynes, a thorough and knowledgeable editor; my parents for the great help they gave me in editing the final draft of Chapter 1; and The Churchill Trust for awarding me a Travelling Fellowship in 1985.

I would also like to thank the many craftsmen who have taught me, especially Fred Whitbread and the Harrises at Wrecclesham, and John Slade. Finally I would like to acknowledge the dedicated support I always receive from my workforce at Whichford Pottery.

PICTURE CREDITS

INDEX

Page numbers in *italics* refer to captions